Business Leadership

Tactical Persuasion Techniques

A Complete Blueprint To Leadership,
Communication, and Management For
The Workplace and Life!

DEREK STANZMA

Business Leadership: Tactical Persuasion Techniques - A Complete Blueprint To Leadership, Communication, and Management For The Workplace and Life! Copyright © 2014 by Derek Stanzma

Disclaimer

ISBN: 0-9939579-1-9
ISBN-13: 978-0-9939579-1-8

PREFACE

Dear Reader,

In scouring articles and books on leadership in the past, I was frequently left behind by the degree of abstraction and theory that I was faced with. Following the pronouncements of most of those books, you had to acquire three or four dozen virtues and countless other characteristics to feel that you were beginning to make headway in pursuit of leadership.

They all made it sound like you aspire to become nothing short of the next Martin Luther King Jr. or Mother Teresa.

That is not how life unfolds. In life, the best that we can do most times is take baby steps in one or two desired directions. Besides, there are one hundred and one different types of leaders (just a whimsical number), so the "leadership" in the books that I read was never more than an amalgam of an extraterrestrial leader –an empty hologram.

Anyway, I wanted to share with you that this book is nothing like that. Instead of listing the string of virtues of a mystery leader, I try to highlight the stories and handful of "aces up their sleeve" that different types of leaders have succeeded in exploiting. From that I try to derive down-to-earth guidelines that can perhaps inspire us. No dictates, no gospel -and definitely no conformity with past books on leaders and leadership. Let us together set our own norms for blazing ahead.

-Derek Stanzma

TABLE OF CONTENTS

CHAPTER ONE
THE STORY OF A BRIT

By the time he took hold of the microphone, he had gained yet more weight and looked like an overstuffed bear. He was more than obese, per the standards of any age, and he bulged out of his clothes at every breath he took. He was also stubby short, smoked incessantly, and was all the time inebriated, hardly ever seen without a balloon glass of cognac in hand. In addition, if you can imagine putting a hockey mask to a bulldog's face, you'd come close to describing what he looked like. All in all, he had the charisma of a wasp.

By the time he took hold of the microphone, he'd

been all his life a natural born narcissist, with everything that mattered in life either made to revolve around him or deemed inconsequential. He was an unapologetic elitist, having been born into a multigenerational family of aristocrats, with the proverbial silver spoon squarely in his mouth. It was rumored that he handled confrontation –i.e. people not falling in line behind him- by threatening and bullying them into submission.

But by the time he got hold of the microphone, he went on to do his thing, and the world was mesmerized. He was no longer stout and bellicose, short-tempered and condescending –he was transformed. He became this vibrant voice that tens of millions of people worldwide clustered around their radios to hear. It was time for Sir Winston Churchill to do his thing, and no one did it better than him. The wasp had turned into someone beloved by all freedom loving people around the globe.

At a time when Britain was inclined to appease – submit- to Hitler, his voice resonated high and defiant:

"We shall go on to the end," he said. "We shall fight on the seas and oceans, we shall fight with

growing confidence and growing strength in the air, we shall defend our Island, whatever the cost may be, we shall fight on the beaches, we shall fight on the landing grounds, we shall fight in the fields and in the streets, we shall fight in the hills; we shall never surrender."

The new Churchill had spoken, and the world took a turn that 5 years later brought about the demise of Nazi Germany.

It has to be said that Churchill, a British political leader and Prime Minister of England in the war years of 1940 to 1945, had all his life been a highly acclaimed and prolific man of the pen (he won the Nobel Prize for literature in 1953 for his six masterful biographical volumes on WWII). Equal to his penmanship were innate faculties that made him a brilliant orator. He would first craft dazzling speeches, and then he would read them with a clarity and intensity that became Churchillian hallmarks.

The description of Sir Winston Churchill –before and after- is intended for us to derive certain conclusions:

What enabled Churchill to become *the* shining light of the war years was not his aristocratic background nor, for sure, his personal lifestyle. If anything, those worked to drag him down, particularly his drinking and narcissism, i.e. excessive interest in himself.

He had three aces up his sleeve however: his vision and foresight in geopolitics, his laser sharp prose and his uniquely resonant speech voice. With those qualities he was able to engage people as far apart as the Indian, European and American continents. For countless millions, he became the ultimate leader in whom their hopes were pinned.

Here are 10 guidelines we can derive from the above:

1. At our end, we are thus urged not to form ironclad theories as to what a leader should look like. We know how we would like a leader to behave, but we've just seen a good example of a leader reaching the pinnacle of his career despite breaking all the rules.

2. However we look physically, or whatever our own attributes, there is always room for us to shine, although we may first have to go on a campaign of self-improvement.

3. A fast way to grow is to examine what aces we may be hiding up our sleeves. We all have strengths, although some of those may still be undeveloped. It's thus time to give those our best attention. If you like something, become good at it. If you're good at it, become an authority on it. The more expertise you gain in any field, the more followers will flock to you.

4. When endeavoring to improve –whatever your direction- it helps to visualize the consequences of your improvements, i.e. what you would become like, how you will be viewed by others, and how it will affect your personal and professional predicaments. Visualizing like this will keep you focused and motivated.

5. Probably Churchill's highest asset was his

communication style. So, work on yours. Start this endeavor with a little self-examination: "How do I speak?" Followed by "How does he speak (someone you respect)?" This can only take you in the right direction.

6. Remember that you speak with your voice, your eyes, your shoulders and the rest of your body including –most significantly- your tone.

7. Another one of the good things you can do for yourself is to be self-aware of how you are accustomed to synchronize between all those instruments of language. Don't go giving mixed signals just because you're not mindful of what your body is doing.

8. Cast your net of friends and admirers wide and deep. You know how it's done on Facebook and Twitter, and it's the same in real life. When you meet new people, be the leader and extend yourself to build an instant rapport. Let them like and trust you. Build on the common bonds that

you can uncover from your past, and if those are scarce, make the first move and open up to the other person, showing that you like and trust them.

9. And when you can't see straight and are possibly confused, go up in an imaginary hot air balloon and examine the far wider landscape, first from 1000 feet, then higher from 5,000 feet. You'd be amazed at how much clearer you'll see. Merge this visualization with that of seeing where you can reach with an effort. That's an unbeatable combination.

10. And finally, persevere. Giving up in the middle of a project —even lifelong projects- is definitely not for you. Find sustenance always, for example from the examples of Steve Jobs and Thomas Edison. You probably know their stories inside out, but they bear repeating from this perspective. In trying to miniaturize the iPhone and get it down to the size we're familiar with, the Steve Jobs team must have tried and failed in hundreds of little experiments. But they persevered and rose to the

top of the hill –to nirvana. Thomas Edison claims that he tried his light bulb 10,000 times before he got it to work, but he persevered, it lit, and up to the top of the hill he went –joining other greats.

CHAPTER TWO
THE NOISE WITHIN

The concept here is simple: it is difficult to achieve much in life, never mind attain exalted leadership, if we can't find answers to the anguish our minds subject us to.

The noise within us rattles us and keeps us in a state of dazed tension. We realize that we do this to ourselves, and yet for the vast majority of us, the answers escape us. For those of us gifted with easy sleep, the darkness of night becomes a partial refuge from the endless barrage of images, emotions, and scripts that we allow to unfold in our minds. We end up disguising it in the less stigmatizing term "stress" or "nervousness".

The speed and alacrity with which the mind processes bits of useless information is frightening. It is thought that we can harbor 30+ thoughts per second, i.e. 1800+ thoughts per minute, and over 2.5 million thoughts a day. For the most part, those are single-shot images that keep popping up from the bottomless reservoir that is our memory. They surface frequently at random, other times in sequences, like fast in-and-out reincarnations from the past.

Our minds are troubled bazaars full of dancing shadows and imprecise thoughts. The incessant thinking process takes us by the scruff of our necks and never lets go. Our minds are rogue chatter boxes, unforgiving and constantly evoking in us fears and emotions associated with sketches from our past, at times going all the way back to when we were children. The world around us becomes senseless, a compilation of successive conflict and soul-impoverished issues to deal with.

In our minds we are constantly evaluating, judging, lamenting and projecting bad things from the past into the future, rehearsing hypothetical dialogues, and simply keeping mental gibberish flowing at the speed of light.

In our minds, we transpose our fears and other emotions −e.g. guilt, frustration, stigmas, and feelings of ineptness- into an imagined future. We aggrandize the issues that trouble us the most, and although on the face of it we aspire for a state free of anxiety, depression and disease, we keep getting increasingly mired in the frenzy of monstrous activity that is inside our minds.

Ever since the beginnings of documented history, several millennia BC, writers, theologians, poets and philosophers have been advocating their methodologies to silence the noise within us. Many realized that bliss −at times referred to as enlightenment or simply peace of mind- can be attained only by subduing the ramblings of the mind, even if only for a few seconds or a minute or two. And as one can imagine, there have been religions, cultures and philosophies devoted almost exclusively to the paradigm of arresting the mind's byzantine ways. It is thus no surprise that millions of people around the world expend endless effort and resources in an ongoing effort to prolong those precious few second or minute or two and turn them into a way of life.

How can we get to extend those unique moments of peace? The demand for modern-day modalities that are touted in the West -modalities that for the most part have been common-place in the East for thousands of years- has increased sequentially in the last couple of decades. It would seem that the more "development" and "progress", the more stressed and stupefied the mindset for most people.

What do you suppose stage fright is all about? When a speaker goes up on stage, the mind goes wild with images of failure and embarrassment. The rampage then frequently feeds on itself, causing the speaker to perform at a fraction of his or her potential.

Just imagine what 10 minutes of uninterrupted deep quiet within us –or one hour or two- would bring about. In his gem of a book titled *"The Power of Now – A Guide to Spiritual Enlightenment"*, Eckhart Tolle gives us an exalting response to our hypothetical. "In those peak moments," he writes, "extraordinary capacities evolve: of love, bodily awareness, vitality, intuition, perception..." Do you see a connection between those "capacities" and our topic of leadership?

What is the answer? How do we attain inner calm? We're bordering there on how do we attain enlightenment? All really good questions for my next book. In this book, my task is to give readers the information and empower them to better deal with some of their brain's compulsive ways.

Briefly though –very briefly- a daily fitness routine, eating and sleeping well, socializing (research studies have found that laughter is a perfect antidote to anxiety), breathing exercises, and the other popular stress-relief modalities of yoga, visualization and meditation come to mind.

So, do you think that Mahatma Gandhi would have had the same reach if he hadn't first tamed his mind? You can ask the same question of most inspiring leaders of the past, and the reason is simple: you cannot give yourself to your preoccupation as a leader when your mind is doing its thing.

CHAPTER THREE
THE HIGH ROAD

The high road is a state of mind, a philosophy, a way of life, a doctrine, a companion and a collection of self-regulating instincts that –for the few- become etched as one mantra on the subconscious mind. You get liberated when you hug the high road, when the difference between right and wrong is in everyone else's mind –hardly ever in yours. The only step up from that lies in further spiritual enlightenment. (Let us not confuse the term "spiritual" with its religious connotation –the one has little to do with the other).

When you hug the high road and are that way liberated, there is no longer the right way and the wrong way, there is only one way that you take as in sleep walking. You don't have to think about it. Instead, your thoughts and emotions can be directed at more significant issues, such as how you can do the most good on that occasion.

Pursuing the high road, as you can already detect, is not for the faint of heart, nor do 99% of our so-called leaders cling to the dictates of the high road. It is not an easy endeavor and is typically a rocky pursuit in which you are on your own.

There frequently is no one other than your inner self to tell you how you're doing, or whether you've veered off course in dealing with something or other. You will be making choices that at times are not the easiest or self-evident. You'll want to reflect and ponder about the best way for you. Here is what the poet Robert Frost had to say in his famous *"The Road Not Taken"* which became better known as *"The Road Less Traveled"* (this is the last of four stanzas):

I shall be telling this with a sigh
Somewhere ages and ages hence:
Two roads diverged in a wood, and I
Took the one less traveled by,

And that has made all the difference.

You see clearly there how the poet agonized over which road to take, the difference between the two divergent roads not easy to detect. In pursuing the high road, you too will at times have to take the road less traveled, prompted solely by your inner fabric –your solid foundation.

For most of us, and for most of our leaders, the high road is a utopic dream that no one can fully undertake. It is just too hard, and the influences against the high road are enormous. You may have to tell a white lie on some occasion, or let someone down in order to help someone else. You may be blamed for the wrongdoings of all around you for –after all- aren't you the leader? Who else is there to blame?

But we begin to get separated on our high road journey, some wielding greater influence than others. That is entirely acceptable. In fact, we all have a role to play, and the only thing we can do is keep working at improving ourselves. That's it: from here on we replace the high road with continuous self-improvement. We can more readily live with that.

Self-appraisals help us in our self-improvement effort. They serve to flush out the bad habits that find their way into your behaviors and mannerisms. From these examinations you can keep track of the degree to which your comportment of late measures up to the standards you have set for yourself. You would naturally want to be as honest as possible in seeking the truth from the following 10 questions:

1. How often do you speak out on impulse, without much thought?

2. How often do you hurt someone in the process, or how often could you have been more delicate in dealing with people?

3. Do you have a personal code for knowing when to speak up, and when to keep something to yourself?

4. Do you find yourself exaggerating or "fibbing" in order to score points?

5. In what situations are you most likely to fib, or

to withhold some of the truth?

6. Do you frequently find yourself gossiping? Do you gossip at someone else's expense, someone who is absent at the time?

7. Do you sometimes find yourself saying one thing and doing another? Do you practice what you preach? Walk the talk?

8. In the last period since your last self-appraisal, did you help "build up" or "tear down" one or more people?

9. Are you comfortable saying no or refusing to partake in something your peers want to do?

10. Do you trust yourself to keep your word, and do others have complete trust in what you say?

There are times when you mean well, but you make a grand –and too ambitious- plan, only to later realize that you neither have the willpower nor the energy to see it through. Other times you find yourself simply running out of steam in the face of troublesome obstacles. Yet more times you simply defer or put off that trip to the gym that you had set your mind on. You then deem it acceptable to simply not do what you had promised yourself you would do. After all, you're not hurting anyone in the process.

Do you see now why we veered away from the high road and into the era of self-improvement? We did mention that the high road was too utopic –too hard- even for our most ardent leaders. But there's lots to do despite that.

One of the fundamental pillars of self-improvement has to do with the word patterns we use. We need to learn to speak with clarity and finality, as in: "We say what we mean and we mean what we say." Everyone knows people who are careless with what they say, who agree to things readily but then never seem to be able to deliver, who exaggerate or speak about things they have no firs-hand knowledge about and who add their own gloss over what they've heard or read. When persons like that are talking about things they have no experience in, using language disparagingly about mutual acquaintances, those individuals forsake all personal credibility. They become a liability, for we are diminished whenever we are exposed to this blatant misuse of language.

We need to avoid lying at all costs, including fibs, white lies, exaggerations and embellishments to stories. In some cultures, white lies and personal integrity are not considered mutually-negating. You can be an avid re-cycler, a charitable person, and an overall good citizen, despite indulging in white lies –when white lies could be an almost acceptable form of twisting the truth in your culture. In the world you function in, lying may thus not necessarily disqualify you from pursuing the higher ends. You should know however that lying is something you do deliberately, intending to deceive.

It is easy to rationalize, convincing yourself that you are lying for a good cause, e.g. to keep from hurting someone's feelings (the most common self-deceit of all), to brighten someone's day, or to avoid explanations that you would rather not have to make. So you ask yourself, who is being hurt with this little lies? No one, therefore you don't feel bad about it.

One of the reasons why our higher goals and lying don't go hand-in-hand is that lying creates a new reality in your mind as well as in your listener's. The first reality is the truth, while the other reality is the one you made your listener live in –the false reality. You will henceforth have to live with that second reality, pushing you to additional lies. Examine carefully how succinctly the Scottish author and novelist, Sir Walter Scott, put it when he wrote:

> *Oh what a tangled web we weave,*
> *When first we practice to deceive!*

The more "tangled webs you weave", the more realities you create, and the more lying you will have to do, bringing upon yourself an energy draining load that will steer you further apart from your fundamental goals. That is why the above 10 questions that were set for your self-appraisal mostly revolved around the power of your words. For you can't have it both ways: you can't be the master of meaningful words while at the same time practicing lying and deceit.

Lying has become so commonplace, most of it

under the pretext that it does no one any harm. To cite a really mundane lie, one that is rationalized so easily, How often have you lied, or asked a coworker to lie on your behalf, when you get a phone call from someone you don't want to talk to ("Tell them I'm not here!")

Moralists have come up with a curriculum for retrieving the power that your words may have lost: speak only what you mean: no exaggerations, gossip, self-deprecating or derogatory language, and use words only for propagating the truth and love. Note that the word "love" was added to the "truth", adding a great deal of complexity to the concept. For frequently, you are not 100% sure as to what the truth is. You may choose not to share a particular truth out of respect for someone else. What would be helpful is a personal code of integrity that you can abide by without second thoughts. Someone thus came up with a simple solution: "There are three questions to ask yourself before you speak the truth. One: Are you certain it's true? Two: Is it necessary? And three: Is it kind?" Ideally, your statements will pass all three tests.

How reliably do you keep your word? How often do you say yes when you know have no intention of following through? How often do you make yourself promises that you conveniently forget about? All of these things may sabotage your ability to achieve your goals. So what can you do to get back into the better moral ground? The first thing would be to examine your language and make the necessary adjustments toward telling the truth, even in small ways. If you are afraid to scorn others with the truth, you may wish to re-examine whether that relationship is one you want to keep. You may indeed have to do some housekeeping and rearrange some relationships in order to pursue your objectives. Shedding some friends may pave the way with replacing them with more honest-loving people.

Everyone knows someone who is thought to be "as honest as they come", meaning with a high sense of integrity. Usually that person stands out as not suffering too many quandaries in their daily life, and as speaking the truth in a measured way. Needless to say, that person is perceived to be "happy".

If in this section of the book you felt you'd been given some direction towards a more fulfilling life, the reason may be that multiple realities that come about as a result of telling lies and half-truths can't be all that appealing to you. You will find yourself to be a much happier person when your words match your intentions and when your actions match your words. You will find yourself sleeping better when at night you won't have to lie awake thinking of what impact something –a half-truth- you told someone will have on them.

Don't forget, you have enough problems with the noise your mind is generating from within. You don't need to ruminate all night about new and distorted lines of thinking.

In addition, As your words gain prominence and become increasingly more meaningful, your reality will begin to reflect that. You will speak from a higher place, and you will use powerful language in the service of your highest options. Above all, when at a crossroads, you will find ways to let love factor in. When that happens, you'll know you are on the right path and headed in the best possible direction. You are truly free when you embark on systematic self-improvement.

CHAPTER FOUR
DON'T LOOK NOW... BUT YOUR BODY PARTS ARE TALKING

We're all familiar with what can be achieved with eye contact −or lack thereof (aka eye aversion). For example, you're strolling down a pavement when coming at you from the opposite direction is this unsavory character, disheveled and looking like he could use a bath. You keep walking, but you instinctively avoid eye contact. In a case like that, eye contact could be construed as an invitation for this person to say or do something that you wouldn't like. More to the point, lack of eye contact, coupled with matching movements from the rest of you, is a clear signal to be left alone.

On another occasion, you are trying to make movements way into the parking lot of a shopping mall on a very busy Saturday afternoon. Blocking your way, partially, is this giant SUV. If he could just move a few inches in the other direction, things would open up nicely for you. So you look out for the driver of the SUV, and you stretch one way, then another, trying desperately to catch his attention so that you could then ask, by way of eye contact, if he would be nice enough to oblige. Finally, he becomes aware of you and throws a glance your way. Bingo, there it was, your chance to let your eyes do the sweet asking.

At times the challenge we face has to do with not knowing what is best for us, i.e. whether to be overtly friendly or remain guarded. The extroverts among us would tend to befriend most newcomers, while some of us who are more introverted would be more selective –or buttoned up. For us the need to feel safe and avoid rejection frequently overrides other considerations.

The muscles that control our facial expressions are called subcutaneous, meaning just under the skin. As each muscle or group of muscles contracts, it makes the corresponding skin move. Now imagine your face gain a particular expression when, for example, the first and third, or the second and fifth group of muscles contract. The result may be clearly different expressions.

It turns out we have 6 muscles moving our eyes, and 33 controlling our faces. Think back to your 10 digit phone number and try to figure out the different permutations you can attain with 10 digits. With 33 variables, you can put on literally countless different messages on your face -for all who can read to read.

I don't have to tell you that some professional poker players have made an unnerving habit of doing precisely that –reading people's faces. By the end of this chapter, you too will have covered some of the ground that leads to 'sensory acuity". This is like the built-in mixer in your stereo system: you'll lower or raise the volume of what you're perceiving, and you'll do it effortlessly.

An aspect that is invariably part of leadership is one's ability to build rapports with different kinds of persons. In trying to build rapports with people, many of us who are reserved don't feel at ease when in the company of new people. We simply don't find it easy to open up and make the small talk that normally gets a relationship going. We tend to wait for the other person to break the ice, and our body language gets all defensive, which in turn does not encourage the other person to come up with sincere and effective overtures. However, even for timid individuals, it is thought that would have a "rapport" experience ten thousand times during their lifetime.

Others are extroverted and have an easy-going gait about them. Their body language is inviting, their manner totally relaxed, and they frequently possess a winning smile which opens all kinds of doors.

You can feel good towards a person like that within minutes of meeting them. You may have much in common or just hit it off based on appearance, voice, mutual friends, humor or any one of other common bonds. As you exchange stories, you quickly find other areas of commonality, binding you further together.

Mirroring the other person's eye contact, facial expressions and emotions is another way of building a rapport that many of us experience occasionally. For that to happen, you must listen to the other person and try to put yourself in their shoes before engaging in a conversation. The listening part is important as a confidence builder, telling the other person that you respect their emotions and sympathize with their viewpoints.

If somebody is talking about a situation in which they experienced pain, anger or joy, the person who is a natural at connecting and rapport building might unwittingly flex the body or gesticulate in sympathy with the talker, thus using body language as what is known as "posture mirroring." This gives a degree of comfort to the other person. Now we have eye contact, facial expressions and posture mirroring in our arsenal.

The voice and tone can also be used to mirror an understanding. Thus if someone raises his or her pitch in excitement over the emotions that they are describing, the easy going rapport builder can mimic those vocal inflections and thereby convey agreement. These ways translate into applause when you are in a theater or listening to a great speaker. If it were fashionable to applaud a new acquaintance as a way of portraying your emotional support, then people would be applauding each other all the time in the streets. Enter more body function.

Building rapport is vital in both our daily as well as our professional lives. How vital can it be? Pushed to an extreme, an extraordinary and much cited example of rapport can be found in Jay Haley's book, *Uncommon Therapy,* about the intervention techniques of the widely acclaimed psychotherapist Milton H. Erickson. Erickson is said to have developed the ability to enter the vision and feelings of his patients and, armed with this rapport, he was able to prescribe effective treatments.

Under more normal circumstances however, someone who is clearly at ease building a rapport with people will doubtless attract better attention from prospective employers who are eager for a new hire to get along well with their other employees.

With a greater facility for rapport building, the new hire is deemed to be better equipped to build productive connections and promptly take over his or her responsibilities without rocking any boats.

Someone who has a great knack for connecting with strangers can almost intuitively create a sense of trust and togetherness upon meeting one or more people. In sales, that seemingly natural rapport building skill receives quick and measurable rewards. Successful sales people have taken rapport building to new heights, developing the tools and skills to gain the trust and confidence of their prospective buyers. And although we can refer to this ability as "intuitive" or "natural", it is frequently cultivated and built-up over time.

In addition, the gift of connecting easily with people is by no means restricted to salespeople. People who are thus endowed, and those who develop the talent, include politicians, business people, managers, venture capitalists, and people in many other walks of life. They all have one trait in common: they are individuals around whom others feel relaxed and understood.

But what if there aren't many things in common to form a bond between two people; or between, for example, a CEO and executives in a different culture; or between a great speaker and an audience outside of his or her usual community. When the Chairman of a large corporation like Bank of America is trying to find an executive for a sensitive and key assignment in Japan, chances are he's not going to find much in common with applying prospects. What the Chairman does however is that he will press hard with alternative rapport building techniques. These can include:

Opening up to the other side with a type of candidness that says to them: "I trust you and am going to tell you some things about me." You can thus find many CEOs starting an interview by saying: "Let me tell you a little about us". It is an ice breaker that puts the other person at ease, and it is the mark of a hugely self-confident leader.

This is making sincerity work for you, but it may not be enough, for they may still find nothing they can correlate with following this candid overture. You can then use a technique known as "isopraxism" which calls for you to reflect back emotions, body language and tone of voice in a mimicking -though not exaggerating- way that gives comfort to the other side.

Self-made millionaires often conduct research on the people they are about to meet with the view to proactively find some areas of mutual interest. They believe that there are commonalities between any two people on earth, and it's just a question of unearthing them. Even when finding out "more" is going beyond Facebook and LinkedIn, they keep at it until they find, or they develop, the thread of a link to serve as an ice breaker and be conducive to a good meeting. It is important, all around, for a top level meeting to start with some easy banter to make everyone smile and relax.

Extroverted and charismatic people at times do themselves an injustice when they simply don't know how or when to apply the brakes to their outpouring of emotions. They keep going with the charm offensive until they hit a wall, typically in the form of a challenge or a problem, at which time they come apart.

You have to know when to express your individuality in a fun way, and when to turn serious in line with what is going on. For a relationship to move up to the rank of "great", both sides have to be multifaceted, and the relationship has to find common ground in more than one area.

We saw above the many expressions that the face's muscles can bring about on someone's face, and we alluded to how the poker player can make sense of the opponents' telltale signals. With sensory acuity, we expand that to all of a person's mannerisms and revealing signals.

The senses that are involved in sensory acuity are primarily:

- Seeing – visually

- Hearing – Auditarily

- Feeling/Touching – Kinesthetically

In the term "sensory acuity", sensory is the study of sight, hearing and touch, and the way we experience the world. And acuity refers to the sharpness or intensification with which our sensory organs receive input. When we're not alert or paying attention, our senses are turned down and missing out on much of what is going on around us, or they can be turned up to pick up on considerably more signals.

Someone who likes to talk a lot and listen hardly ever is not interested either in giving out proper signals or in interpreting anyone else's

When we are in a conversation with someone, we are often simply not paying full attention to the signs that the person is generating: body language, gaze, tone of voice, twitching of the eyes, posture, perspiration and a lot more. We are just listening to their voice, and we are consequently often jumping to the wrong conclusions because of our inattentiveness.

The lesson we can derive from that is not to form definitive impressions or conclusive thoughts about matters when your acuity is turned down. And the other side of that would be to always turn up your acuity if you're in an important meeting. Sensory acuity may pick up idiosyncrasies that might make all the difference for you. This turning down and turning up we likened earlier to the mixer on your stereo, except that in this case it doesn't reflect on volume (decibels) but sharpness (pixels).

When your acuity is turned down, your mind is still registering many of the signals that your sensors are missing out on. For example, you can be in a conversation with someone who seems friendly, but you leave that conversation with ill feelings. Your subconscious would be telling you that something was not right, and you only wish you had paid more attention, for with sensory acuity, you might have noticed such incongruences.

In addition, people can say one thing when their body language is saying something different. They're acting odd. It's important in such cases that you turn up your acuity and believe less in what you're hearing and more in the indirect signs you're receiving: poise, tone of voice, shifting eyes, etc.

If you're a leader or business manager, you're all

the time gaging the ongoing dynamics in your staff or followers. You don't necessarily go by what you hear or see superficially, for that may leave you in a misguided position or open to unwanted surprises. You open yourself up to the more heightened input that sensory acuity can give you.

Sensory acuity also applies to language. In an important meeting, you can bet that the Chairman of a large corporation would have his or her sensory acuity turned up, trying to listen to incongruences between the words or language people use as against all the other signs they are emitting. Or, conversely, trying to pick up on telltale negative words such as "I'll try", or "I'll do my best", when the tone is saying that the other side is not being sincere.

Sensory acuity naturally also plays an important role in rapport building, for your heightened senses will tell you if someone's language and behavior are moving in a congruent manner. They will highlight possible inconsistencies for you to ponder.

To develop your acuity, you must first do your best to turn down the chatter that your mind is producing all the time (per our earlier chapter on "The Noise Within"). You then train yourself to simply absorb what the senses are producing with as little interpretation as possible. When your senses are heightened, there should be not much time left for forming impressions or thoughts. There is time enough, later, for all the interpretations.

In short, with sensory acuity you can develop faster and more adroitly as manager, leader, public speaker, student and person of the world. You amplify the input that your senses produce, and you learn the different signals that people emit all the time, thus gaining a valuable edge in life.

In the science known as neuro-Linguistic Programming (NLP), one learns that the actual verbal elements of a conversation carry much less weight than non-verbal elements. How much less? The Professor of Psychology, Albert Mehrabian, gave the following ratios for what influences us in liking or disliking someone we've just met:

- 7% linguistic, i.e. words and language

- 38% tonality, i.e. the tone of voice

- 55% physiological, i.e. mostly body language and physiology

Thus under NLP, we perceive the non-verbal world with a greater level of awareness. It breaks down the input we receive into sensory or internal, i.e. changes in the visual, hearing, and feelings, and external, i.e. facial, body language and changes in tone.

NLP uses the term "calibration" to refer to the detection of incongruences or inconsistencies that are coming from another person, particularly from the person's body movements and tone of voice where the tone of voice (e.g. lively) is signaling something different to the body language (e.g. edgy).

Thus students of NLP learn to work on and develop their own sensory consciousness so that they may readily detect subtle changes in someone else's changes in emitted signals, particularly when such changes are fine and normally hard to detect, requiring a considerable turning up of sensory acuity.

Some people would have developed a knack for "reading" other people, e.g. being able to tell when someone has an ulterior motive or is not telling the whole truth. These are probably extroverted people who might have thus naturally developed some calibration skills. Sensory acuity doesn't work as well for someone who is introverted, for their awareness experience in the ways of people would have been limited.

NLP points to "visual" clues, or things you see in another person's body language, with possible slight variations occurring in breathing, pupil expansion, skin tone, lower lip modulations, and tiny muscles movements. More readily observed changes in body language might include tilting back or forward, crossing legs and arm folding.

Auditory signals would be those you hear when someone else is speaking to you. You would pay attention to their tone, volume, voice clarity, pausing, how fast they're talking and, finally, the actual words they use (the 7% linguistic factor!)

Boosting visual awareness to the point where you can handily detect minute changes in the person's color of skin or breathing patterns is hardly an easy feat. However, people who register for NLP courses claim that with practice, sharpening your skills becomes achievable in not too long a period.

One of the NLP exercises for boosting your sensory

awareness would have you sit and remain focused at the center of an object while expanding your peripheral vision to see clearly objects at both extremities. This wide angle view enables you to become aware of the entire field of vision, while its reverse, tunnel vision, gives you a narrower yet more focused field of vision.

Here is an NLP process that aims at expanding your visual awareness. If you follow and practice it, you'll be able to acquire the ability to sense what is going on around you in greater detail:

- Sit comfortably, concentrate on a spot on the wall ahead of you and breathe calmly.

- Now widen your sight so that you see half a yard either side of the spot while you remain concentrated on the spot. Then from half a yard go to one yard, and then to two yards, while always remaining focused on the spot.

Following this exercise, many people found that they had acquired a relaxed form of added alertness of the visual field. This revealed to them that some people are more revealing than others, and that the body language that people have differ widely from one person to the next.

This process is particularly important for leaders and persons who aspire to become leaders. The more people you bring into the fold, the more you will need to decipher who is sincere and who is not. If you're a department head interviewing applicants all the time, imagine the advantages you would have if you could read a little beyond what a future employee is telling you. If you're a venture capitalist seeking to partner up with different emerging entrepreneurs, you would do well to make sensory acuity part and parcel of your due diligence.

In many other walks of life, including everyday life, it is important to remain alert to the possibility of incongruences coming out of a person you're talking to. They may be telling you "That's wonderful," when their skin color has gone pale, and they are breathing harder. You don't need to interpret anything on the spot, but simply let this early awareness prompt you to a heightened state of acuity to see if there are more inconsistencies to come from that person.

In business, people go to extremes to please a buyer, including promising delivery schedules that they claim "would be no problem". This would be a vital time to have your senses turned up all the way, for if they are lying or not telling the whole truth, your business could suffer. So, with heightened sensors, you might look them in the eye and just have them repeat to you that they would have no problems with the delivery schedule. In a case like that, you might easily spot an inconsistency –sufficiently to put you on high alert and save you later headaches.

CHAPTER FIVE
SPEAKERS & LEADERS

Meet Jenny and Dr. Conrad

Here is how speech night at Jenny's college unfolded, narrated by Jenny herself. I only did a little paraphrasing and changed the names. Jenny's story, narrated by Jenny herself, combines between coaching sessions on public speaking, featuring Dr. Conrad, her teacher and mentor, and a much-touted speech by Dr. Conrad. Here's Jenny:

With my own speech date looming ever so closely, the adrenaline was flowing freely inside of me, and I was in a relentless state of nervousness, even with another 10 days before my turn came up. I was due to give a Graduation speech in 10 days' time for students, faculty and parents.

We had discussed that many times in public speaking class, how stage fright engulfs a speaker way before getting up on stage. Your mind plays dirty tricks, making you see only the possibility of mental freezing, dismay, embarrassment and letting your family and friends down.

I was so lucky and excited at the opportunity of watching and listening to Dr. Conrad, my expectations heightened by everything that we had spoken about and practiced in class with regard to public speaking. I would listen to and see his teachings in action. He was such a gentleman, and I sincerely hoped that he would shine tonight, as was expected of him.

It was said that tonight he would speak about "empathy", though I had no idea from what perspectives. We had harped on and on in class about the importance of choosing a theme. He would say things like, "Themes don't grow on trees, they start by being little tantalizing ideas, and then they build from the middle out. You don't embark by figuring out what *your opening words will be, nor by fixating on the turns and twists of your narrative. You have the basis for a theme, and you begin working it until it starts gaining in clarity –until at one point it grows from vague topic to something that suddenly lights you up, something you feel is beginning to talk to the passions in you. That's when it's time to push forward and develop a solid plan for your presentation –how you want to handle it from beginning to end- and only then can you go up and speak about it." He would also counsel us like this: "To remain focused, ask yourself every now and again why you are going to all this trouble –why you are doing all this. If the fire is still there, that would be your sign that you're on the right track."*

For added emphasis, I remember Dr. Conrad saying something like, "Do your best thoughts come when you're on fire, or do they come as a result of passionate labor and development? Did Martin Luther King, Jr. start with the phrase "I have a dream", or did he work his way up to it by feeling passionately about his people's plight? Naturally, we don't know, but for the rest of us would-be great speakers and leaders, it is best to assume that it came to him at the right time in the right sequence after working tirelessly on his speech."

Although Dr. Conrad was probably in his early sixties, he had an athletic gait about him and looked energetic, genuine and kind. With two of my classmates who were tugging along, I made my way towards groups of people waiting to be asked to take their seats. We wanted to find out what they were saying about our coach, although we really had not much to worry about as he was very popular on campus. He had two PhD's, one in Philosophy, and one in Computer Science. Not bad I thought, having spent the last months cramming my head off for a mere Master's. We knew him to have a wide-ranging and deep intellect. One of my other teachers told me yesterday that when Dr. Conrad will speak, he will probably evoke an unprecedented level of positive introspection, elevating his audience and filling them with unfettered optimism –which, it so happened, is precisely what empathy is supposed to do.

My friends and I thought that the room was filling up to its maximum capacity of 800 people, and we'd been determined to get there early so as to secure good seats.

Empathy, I thought, trying to break it down in my mind into all that it could entail. In view of his acumen and his chosen theme, we promptly decided that it would have to be a motivational presentation, an all-inspiring one which, for us, made the evening all the more exciting. After all, that was smack in the middle of what we were studying.

I was in the middle stages of writing a paper on self-assessment for my Master's, so I could hardly wait to see if Dr. Conrad's talk would touch on my subject. I was tossing and turning between the concepts of self-esteem, self-compassion, and self-worthiness, and I was trying hard to form opinions as to the precise differences between those. I was therefore hoping for a real bonus if our coach would bring those up in an analytical way.

People were milling about when he showed up, about half an hour before "prime time". He was suddenly talking to a bunch of professors not far from where we were standing. "Engaging the audience", Jenny thought to herself, "working the room". She had read and learned in class that chatting with one or two groups in the audience before a speech would make it easier for the speaker to understand and relate to the audience.

In fact researching and finding out as much as one could about one's audience would be a necessary step when forming the content of the speech. You want to always fine tune the messages in your presentation and render them relevant to that particular audience. Mixing with one or two groups who were milling about just before the speech leaves the speaker with the impression that the audience consists of friendly and sympathetic people, which goes some way towards lessening the nervousness when it's time to start. In his speech, the speaker might even say something like: "I had a chance to chat with Mr. Spencer a few minutes ago and was happy to learn that there are many people in the audience who..." Again, this is all towards breaking the ice.

When he cracked up in laughter, as he did more than once, his face broke out in an inviting and highly charismatic way. He quickly came across like a man of great "non-judgmental understanding", aka empathetic –again- a leadership quality that enables the person to feel through you all the way to the various issues that you were facing.

My friends and I made our way across the bodies until we were by his side. He looked me in the face, gave me a big smile, and there it was, like an angel's touch, a lifting of the spirit, a euphoric sense of "good things are sure to come your way".

I crossed my fingers in the sign of good luck, and he smiled back again. He seemed totally relaxed, although underneath that façade, I assumed there would be even a smidgen of turmoil

Then it was time. He was behind the podium, clearing his throat to test the acoustics, tidying up his little index cards. He then gave a slow and deliberate gaze around the audience, as if preparing to talk to them individually, his warm smile never leaving his face for an instant.

I waited impatiently to see how he would handle stage fright, but the man was as calm as a sleepy landscape out in the hills. He had obviously left his nerves on other stages prior to this one. The way he taught stage fright was to accept and then tame it. "Even the best speakers used stage fright to get pumped with adrenaline and then to perform at their best." He had frequently said. "They would be listless without the stress of "prime time".

"If you're physically fit, and you practice until you truly own your topic, you can tame the nervousness." Dr. Conrad would counsel. "For an ideal posture, and for the ability to make your voice boom from deep in your diaphragm and lungs for 30 minutes without respite, you had better be perfectly fit. In addition, run for two or three miles on the day of the speech. That will clear your mind nicely."

"As for being prepared," He would tell us, "practice is the leverage that can take you from average to great, and from great to spectacular. It is the transformative tool that gives you clout of the type that you would never be able to muster, no matter how intuitively talented you may be, without it. And while there are practicing methods of various types, the rehearsing we're talking about turns your speech into an internal dialogue —so that you may deliver free of disturbances, with calm and brilliant timing, as though you were talking to your best friend." He would give us short overnight assignments that required that we practice from notes, then from index cards, in front of a mirror and, the next day, in front of the 20 people in the class.

He opened with a series of short jokes that in essence were self-deriding. The jokes were about his parents' aspirations for him during the free-wheeling seventies, and how he had "let them down".

We had spoken countless times in class about the first minute or two, how you had to grab your audience, and the use of "hooks" like humor, a story, an outlandish quotation, or even one or two questions that had funny answers. Humor and a short and insightful story always came out ahead, and there he was now using not only humor, but linking it to a personal story about his family. Anyway, whatever one can say about it, it was brilliant, for the audience laughed out loud at his opening remarks, a sure sign that they would give him smooth sailing from that point on.

The other thing that came to mind was that Dr. Conrad must have practiced his jokes meticulously. "Don't ever improvise with humor," he would say, "for a word or two out of place would be enough to cause you great problems." Then he added, "Don't start a story either if you haven't practiced it thoroughly. A story has to have an opening, then some tension in the middle, and finally a nice unwinding at the end. It is easy to leave an audience suspended in mid-air if you can't tell the story properly from beginning to end."

He spoke slowly in measured terms, his sentences ringing with clarity, making sure that everyone in the auditorium could hear and understand him.

My friends and I were not in the least surprised at the degree of accomplishment his speech-making had risen to. We watched his every move and listened intently to how he laid out his presentation. He was evidently making his way through a carefully crafted plan that engulfed all aspects of his talk, including his personal story at the beginning, and how he linked back to it at the end.

Needless to say, Dr. Conrad developed his theme of empathy as masterfully as could be expected. He spoke of love and compassion in exalted terms, bringing us all to a tingling state of elevated awareness as to the human condition, and what each one of us could do to elevate it. He reminded my friends and I of what he would say about public speaking requiring disciplines of the type that can help people overcome big hurdles throughout their personal lives. Whether in one-on-one meetings (for example in interviews and many sales situations), or pitching to a group (for example to partners, boardroom members or venture capitalists), or facing larger groups (for example congregations and miscellaneous audiences), it is the same speech-making grounding that can open doors and make their goals more attainable.

"People who deliver presentations that resonate, wield influence and have lasting impact have learned how to add bountiful measures of discipline in all facets of their lives and particularly when it comes to posture, eye contact and a charismatic presence in the important meetings of their everyday lives." Dr. Conrad didn't say that, but knowing him, he might have said it.

CHAPTER SIX
INTUITION & SPIRITUAL AWAKENING

Guilt & the Rewards of Positive Thinking

Have you ever stopped to take measure of the baggage we carry around, the dead weight that gives us the crouch in our posture and the anguish in the head? Guilt attaches to us from infancy, and we then proceed to accumulate layer after layer of it, unaware of its insidious ways. As we develop, all kinds of stressors pile on: inherited predispositions to anxiety and disease, psychological, family and cultural-related stressors, not to mention employment and financial stress. The twin-headed monster of guilt and stress hides inside us like a sticky parasite that becomes hard to dislodge.

Some of us make the above burden worse by adopting negative attitudes. We carry the stress on our wrinkled foreheads and go about with a doomsday attitude, pessimism clouding everything we do. One path to healing requires some repair work to our self-compassion, not that tough a barrier to cross. After all, there are things that we're great at, perhaps as parents, friends, spouses, employees or lovers. All we need to do is turn our frame of mind around so that we recognize that we are indeed worthy of having a reasonable break in life, a fair shake —and a fair standing in society. How we view our worthiness can in turn become the base upon which we build a new balance in life. When we view ourselves compassionately, it follows that we may view others with equal benevolence and before we know it, people will start sensing us in that new light.

5 measures to enhance self-compassion

Note that we are not dealing with "self-esteem", for that has a higher standard requiring that the person have accomplishments and be successful, e.g. as a leader or such. Self-acceptance is an interim step that is relatively easier to achieve, although at its base can be deeply rooted psychological factors.

1. Start by bringing awareness into the fore. What did you feel you were unworthy of? Did your culture, religion, or social upbringing bring that about? Do you have ethical reasons for feeling that way –did you wrong somebody?

2. Researchers have found that people with self-compassion who admit to having made mistakes in life are highly motivated to make amends and excel –better in that respect than people with high self-esteem whose ego can be "shattered" by failure. So look your mistakes in the eye and go to work.

3. Start a dialogue -preferably in writing in a journal- with the pain, guilt, and other negative aspects of how you see yourself. Write about what you are feeling, how you want to change your ways. Keep the standards attainable and the goals within reach.

4. Go for a mighty move: help someone in your circle of acquaintances who is less fortunate

than yourself. Do some volunteer work, for that can be rewarding.

5. Go into the outdoors as often as you can, and walk with people who are boisterous and who laugh a lot. Try to talk, mix, and laugh as much as possible. Isolationism is not your best friend, nor is the company of other cynics, or doomsday-scenario types.

Open your mind to intuition

Intuition is always described as the "sixth" sense that is in all of us. Cultivating that sense opens incredibly enriching doors in our lives: doors to getting closer to our goals, to creativity, happiness, feeling free and to a higher awareness of our spirituality. This section aims at bringing that entire dimension to you, helping you to bring out the full potential of your intuitive powers.

Before you allow your "logical" mind to pooh-pooh and shut out this marvelous life companion, see what these 5 famous people had to say about intuition:

1.   *"Your time is limited, so don't waste it*

living someone else's life," says Steve Jobs. "Don't be trapped by dogma – which is living with the results of other people's thinking. Don't let the noise of others' opinions drown out your own inner voice. And most important, have the courage to follow your heart and intuition. They somehow already know what you truly want to become. Everything else is secondary." **Steve Jobs**

2. "There is no logical way to the discovery of these elemental laws. There is only the way of intuition, which is helped by a feeling for the order lying the appearance." **Albert Einstein**

3. *"Once the information is in the 40% to 70% range, go with your gut. Don't wait until you have enough facts to be 100% sure, because by then it is almost always too late."* **Colin Powell**

4. *"I think we need the feminine qualities of*

leadership, which include attention to aesthetics and the environment, nurturing, affection, intuition and the qualities that make people feel safe and cared for." **Deepak Choprah**

5. "Sex and beauty are inseparable, like life and consciousness. And the intelligence which goes with sex and beauty, and arises out of sex and beauty, is intuition." **D. H. Lawrence**

You can be skeptical all you want about intuition, but do yourself a favor, don't shut it out –don't be cynical on the subject. Cynicism is the absolute enemy –it can eat away at your self-esteem like a relentlessly corrosive compound.

The fact that many of us choose to ignore this extra-sensory capability speaks loudly to what our fast-paced world has come to. We eat foods that have been genetically modified and laden with dyes, preservatives and other poisons, and we submit to an endless stream of pharmaceuticals to quench our pains and discomforts, and yet when it comes to our intuitive energies, we view them with distrust, brainwashed by the Western socio-economic environment that seems perpetually fixated on the priorities of indulgence and materialism. For the sake of your self-improvement and further enlightenment, break away from all that and broaden your mind's horizons. Bring into your life a new confidence in your intuitive energies and gain an invaluable companion for life.

Intuition and leaders

Intuition is a personal tool that can direct you towards the best outcomes in life. But for that to happen, you have to first recognize it among the many influences that compete for your attention, particularly at important moments in your life. You have to be able to see beyond the smokescreens that your mind puts up.

And even when you recognize it, you have to encourage it, trust it and let it show you the path forward. Those are critical requirements, but so are the amazing rewards. The requirements involve discipline and effort on your part. In other words, reliable intuition doesn't grow on trees.

Intuition starts as being that "gut feeling" or

"hunch" that you might get from sources that you cannot see and do not comprehend. But intuition develops into much more than that.

For spiritual beings, intuition crosses the trajectory from gut feelings to divine knowledge. To understand the meaning of spiritual concepts such as "divine", intuition is that orderly information that you acquire without any logical effort on your part.

Intuition appears from unknown origins, and its appearance takes many forms: for some it might be sensed vividly, a knotting in the stomach or a stiffening of one or more muscles, while for others it might appear in more subtle forms, like a feeling, a knowledge, a sense of suddenly being elated or worried or perplexed.

You can summon your intuitive powers only after you've worked at it and made progress in the art of distinguishing and trusting your intuition. That is not difficult, and it does not require any prior experience. All you need to do is open your eyes and shut out the ramblings of the world around you.

Leaders rely on their inspiration to "read" the

energy when they enter a room, or to detect what is in a person's heart that they are conversing with. This quality is essential to a leader's traits. A leader's followers are in turn inspired by their leader's insights that seem to come naturally to him or her. In order that you experience inspiration you must first:

- Rid yourself of all cynicism and open your mind to a leap of faith and consciousness; silence that loud-mouthed inner critic who likes to bat down all your unusual ideas.

- Learn to discern intuitive energies and acknowledge their innate origin (like you acknowledge that trees do fall and make noises in the middle of the forest even though you don't see them); don't always try to assign logical explanations that don't make much sense. How many times has your logical (left) brain been wrong?

- Quiet down the noise within you so that you may hear *the* voice that summons –your intuition

- Cultivate your intuition and nurture its growth –take it from "hunch" to inner guidance

- Practice trusting and following your intuition

What does a stockbroker rely on when he makes 100 trades in a minute or two? You might say he relies on experience, but frequently there is no background experience. For example, when Einstein was into his mathematical formulas, he was smack within uncharted terrain. No prior experience there, only his intuition. Why did he follow certain patterns that lead him to the result he sought and not other patterns? You've got it –he followed his intuition.

And when Bill Gates and his associates were writing the codes for Microsoft, do you think they went through every option at every crossroads? Never, for that would have taken them forever. Because of sharpened intuitions, they were able to make quantum leaps forward, dramatic short cuts that could not have been foreseen purely on the strength of their intellect.

Switch your headlights on

Anyone aspiring for self-improvement and a leadership role in his or her community should periodically make it a habit to switch their headlights on. Imagine you're driving down a winding road at night with your regular lights on. You can only see up to where your lights illuminate the road. That is how you are normally navigating the twists and turns of life, including any effort you are making towards self-improvement. Then –as if for the first time- switch your headlights on. The new vista is awe-inspiring. You never figured as much, and you'll now be much better equipped for life and the pursuit of happiness.

Try to shut out the "street" noise and dampen your own baggage –you know, the one you carry around- and perceive life through your new prism. You'll be amazed at the insights that will come your way when you do that, and how much more alive your senses will be.

When you keep the headlights on for life, i.e. when you invite in and nurture your intuition, you will witness ahead of you the unraveling of some of what you previously held as sacred principles. You will begin to grasp the predicament that Man finds himself in, and you will want to help. The leader in you will start emerging, and your path will have been set.

When you feel you want to help, that is a sure sign that you are also on your way to spiritual enlightenment. Your true compassion, pushed down up to that moment by the senseless buzzing in your mind, comes out in full bloom. When you view what's ahead through the new prism, your goodness will take over as if by magic. You will suddenly see through the haze and marvel at how stunning the universe that you belong to is. Hopefully, you will see nature spread itself out gloriously, and you will feel some kind of subliminal fusion with it, as if you were one with it.

Baby steps is the way to go

These days people want instant gratification, or else forget it! People can't be bothered to learn anything that may take more than a few days to master. They expect immediate outcomes from everything they attempt, even open-ended concepts such as positive thinking, self-improvement, leadership virtues and much more.

Well, things never happen this way. You can't

magically develop the muscular body of your dreams just by fantasizing about it. And you can't attain a meaningful level of spiritual awakening and leadership by daydreaming about it.

Laziness, lack of focus and too much negative thinking prevent people from pursuing the high road and its various outcomes. If results do not appear immediately, people become disappointed and lose faith. In inventing the light bulb —we've given this example many times, but what better example?- Thomas Edison didn't readily give up after a day or two —he is thought to have made 10,000 attempts before getting it right.

Here is what Mahatma Gandhi recommended:

"I have not the shadow of a doubt that any man or woman can achieve what I have, if he or she will make the same effort, and have the same hope and faith." **Mahatma Gandhi**

Developing the power of focus and determination, overcoming negative habits, seeking purpose and acquiring the virtues of the high road that we discussed, these require work over time, just like any other worthwhile endeavor. You must not think of this needed work as a tough, mountainous road. Instead, think of it as a series of incremental, baby steps, each one producing its own rewards and laying the ground for the next step.

Spiritual awakening has nothing to do with religion, and it is for everyone. Like intuition, it needs to "awaken" or be discovered and pursued, and once that pursuit is developing, it produces a more harmonious life that is free of fear and anxiety. Once again, what one has to do in order to attain some degree of spiritual awakening is to remove everything that hides this knowledge. In other words, you would need to:

- Silence your mind and open yourself to your spirituality

- Get rid of false concepts and beliefs that have lodged inside your mind over time

- By wiping out your notions of who you are and of the world around you, you increase your awareness of your real self, beyond the ego

- Drop negative thinking altogether, including erroneous beliefs and let your inner self come out and shine

- You must be able to "see" beyond your ego personality

Before you start thinking that this is beyond your capabilities, have a look at the rewards:

- You will have a much deeper understanding of who you are

- You will know an inner peace like never before, together with feelings of engagement with the entire universe

- You will not be affected by life's whims

- You will boost your inner strength and confidence and your ability to overcome negative thinking and circumstances

We all tend to view ourselves and the rest of the world with multiple pairs of sun glasses on. As we remove each pair, we have a new and clearer view of our surroundings. Spiritual awakening requires that you remove the sun glasses one step at a time. This will enable you to have new visions that will also inspire you to take the next step.

You can do the required work without making drastic changes in your life. All you need is to want to take that path and to persevere. Here are some tips that you may find useful:

1. Learn to silence the noise inside your mind and focus as best you can. (Have you noticed how many references we've made to the noise inside your mind?) Practice breathing or meditation to help you with that.

2. Try to find and associate with individuals who have gone on the road to spiritual awakening.

3. Try to see the truth in that you are a spirit with a body and not the other way around. This is a prerequisite to real advancement.

4. Positive thinking is essential: there is a bright side to everything; you are stronger than your circumstances.

5. Marshal your attention to where you want it rather than letting it wander and do what it wants.

6. Do your best to be tolerant, patient, tactful and considerate. Acquire all the noble traits of a leader "in development", particularly those involving your integrity and the high road.

CHAPTER SEVEN
TACTICAL PERSUASION

In theory, the more democratic the societies we live in, the bigger the influence we exert through our vote, through the lobbies that represent us and by means of the funds that we may from time to time contribute in pursuit of some say in what goes on.

It doesn't always work out in as clear-cut a manner as that though. The influence of big money often trumps our little voting power. the most influential entities in the US are the pharmaceutical, farming, banking, tobacco, manufacturing, legal and other influence-wielding industries that spend billions annually on their lobbies and on the general electorate in an attempt to influence who gets elected into the powerful positions in government. They thus get to influence how our elected officials stand on the issues of interest to them, and they get to have a significant say in the writing of legislation.

There is hardly a lobby or interest group in the country that doesn't have an office in our capital, and there is a whole street, K Street, that is known to contain almost nothing but lobbyists. Many of the lobbyists there get annual salaries and bonuses in the millions of dollars. The amounts thus spent on each election cycle in the US have risen from tens of millions of dollars for each of the two main parties a couple of decades ago to an astronomical $6.5 billion in advertising and other influencing mechanisms in the midterm elections of November 2014. This figure will also doubtless be exceeded come the Presidential elections of 2016.

Influence by Persion

Influence has many faces, and we are fielding a constellation of them on a daily basis. No matter where we turn, someone is trying to influence us: to buy a product, take advantage of a "sale", go see a particular movie, and the barrage goes on endlessly.

Even people leaving reviews for books, restaurants, movies and practically everything else nowadays wield influence over us. These days it seems we can't make a move without first checking Yelp and other review boards.

People appeal to our sense of morality –here's what's good for you- or they shower us with potential rewards -$50 off if you buy today. On television, we are being "shown" the way, all day long, for how we can be like our sports heroes, or like a beautiful model who promises us that we too can lose 30 lbs. in 3 weeks. In their salesmanship, companies will also appeal to our sense of "self-actualization", a concept developed by Psychologist Abraham Maslow. "...This tendency might be phrased as the desire to become more and more what one is, to become everything that one is capable of becoming." In other words, we're being sold on our own potential, if only we were to buy a product or service.

We thus find ourselves day and night in the cross hairs of marketers, developers, charities, distributors, ad people and many other categories of folks who have nothing but our so-called best interests in mind.

Information "overload" becomes another factor that influences us increasingly as we get bombarded with choices and plays on our emotions and feelings of guilt. It makes us worry about regretting decisions we make and hesitate in the face of being tugged at from different directions. This tends to add to our already stressed frame of mind which, in turn, might make us defer decision-making until we are "clearer" –or until we check out what other people had said in Yelp and reviews!

Naturally, leaders are occupied with influence as well, though not for obvious commercial reasons. In fact, influence is the bread and butter of leadership, and without influence, leadership would wither and die.

Effective leaders first attract, then they persuade,

and then they wield their influence, frequently by way of an unspoken call-to-action that carries the "come join me" insinuation, or openly: "let's all combine to raise some money for that charity", or "let us pray" if you're in church. All of those and an assortment of others constitute a leader's brand of invitation, as well as the circumstances.

In order to implement steps or policies that are perceived as essential, leaders have to get "their flocks" to follow suit. They have to exert their influence –in different strengths or seriousness, depending on the nature of the demands being made of the followers. The demands can be to alter opinions, behavior, attitudes and visions among other possible goals. Leaders wield influence in a specific direction in order to bring about change.

Leaders may find themselves in need of influencing others, including other leaders both below and above them in rank, some totally unknown to them and on whom they have no formal authority. For example, a middle level manager in a complex multinational setting may be asked to create a team of five people, including two executives in Japan, in order to troubleshoot an irritating problem.

With the rise of "virtual teams" like that, managers have had to sharpen their skills in the fields of building rapports, influencing others, persuading (including negotiating), networking, using "command-style" methods to assert their leadership and preempt obstacles. They may never have met their counterparts in Japan, and they certainly have no official authority over them.

They were chosen for this task because they are leaders –resourceful, charismatic, focused, and good at wielding authoritative influence.

Leasers choose different tactics to be effective in wielding their influence. For example, soft or hard tactics may be the first choice, depending on whether they absolutely must have a result or they can leave the other person or flock with some maneuvering room. When necessary, leaders can switch from soft tactics to additional assertiveness and a harder posture. At the back of a leader's thinking always is the degree of strain that he or she would like to put on a particular relationship. In fact, in their quest to influence others, leaders have at their disposal an entire array of tactics from inspirational, consultation, rational or personal appeals and assertive or hard.

Similarly, in response to the influence that is being wielded at them, the followers can resist, comply or commit. Even followers have a range of responses within these categories. For example, they can resist softly, perhaps by asking the leader for more time or to modify his or her stance, ignore, delay, or rebut with an outright refusal.

There are times also when a department head with strong leadership qualities is faced with a gradual slippage in his department's performance. He thus needs to gather his staff and probably exercise several tactics simultaneously. He would need to cajole, motivate, coach, demonstrate, put people on notice and ultimately perhaps also use a threatening tenor to ensure that he has everyone's complete compliance.

From the above we learn that leadership is not just about living an exemplary life and amassing a whole slew of virtues, it is also like the art of wrestling. You have to master all the moves and become adept at switching over comfortably from one to the other in pursuit of your ultimate goals. If you apply the inappropriate tactic, you stand to have your influence boomerang back at you.

When you work in a team, whether across borders or within the same office, you have to rely on multiple people below and above you to maintain and grow your level of leadership. Ultimately a corporate CEO has to get along and be persuasive with his Board of Directors as well as shareholders. For those reasons and many more, tactical persuasion and personal influence are critically needed skills. You have to be able to affect other peoples' actions, opinions and attitudes. Getting compliance from followers is frequently not sufficient for you to deliver on your goals. What you need is peoples' commitments, and for that you have to be adept at applying moves from an entire array of possible tactics.

In today's unsettled economy and with other variables always disrupting the best laid plans, nothing replaces true and definitive commitment, particularly in the workplace. This kind of bond gives you the freedom to move forward, knowing that your followers won't turn into back-stabbers at the slightest provocation. They will endorse you and support your plan. It might be that at the behest of your superiors, you are in the middle of implementing a big organizational or other change. You want people to buy into your change, not act as impediments all along. You want to delegate, and have people in your flock themselves in turn delegate. You may have been asked to cut down on your division's budget, or to let 10% of your people go. These are tough decisions asked of you, and they require the toughest of tactics. This is where you brandish all your might and leave no room for misinterpretation or wishy-washiness when it comes to your authority.

When you use the right tactics and persuade people to follow your lead, and they assume a posture of genuine commitment, you will find that your relationships will start to improve. Your office mates will smile more often and will show you superior work. The reason is that it is just as unsettling for followers as it is for leaders to have vagueness encroach into an important relationship. In other words, with final commitment, they will relax to the whole issue and let you handle the bigger matters of the workplace.

How to go about attaining this bliss? One way would be to use logical tactics, i.e. try to make sense with logical arguments. You reason with objectivity, giving factual evidence and offering practical alternatives. If dealing with workplace issues, you explain what "going against the grain" would imply to you, your followers, other people in the organization, and what other repercussions may come about.

You can add a personal tactic to that, making it a personal logical appeal, bringing in the argument, for example, of how a decision one way or the other may affect someone's long term career. Alternatively, when you know someone well, you can use emotional tactics, connecting your message to individual outcomes or goals. You can link your message to a vision that the person understands better and appreciates. This is particularly useful if you're trying to delegate a cumbersome or complex task. You can describe the task with enthusiasm and show appreciation when the first moves are accomplished.

Yet another alternative, a highly effective one in an office setting, is to build a link between your message, the person you are trying to influence, and other people in the organization. In a sense you're saying that if your follower gives you a firm commitment, it would help a whole load of other people around the office. You may ride on the wave being created by your top

Management, for instance, to draw alliances that they would be happy with.

Naturally, the best tacticians use combinations of tactics. As we mentioned earlier, the more influential a person, particularly in a practical, down to earth setting like the workplace, the more adept he or she will be at shifting between tactics naturally and with positive flair.

Leaders know all about tactical persuasion. They may not know it as such, but they practice the moves deftly. Otherwise they wouldn't be leaders.

Social Media Influencers

Social media have given the individual a reach – and influence- as never before, one to rival traditional media outlets. Take any field that may be of interest to the average person, e.g. one of the sciences, and you might easily find out that social media moguls discuss the ins and outs of that field just as much, if not more, than academicians. Who are these moguls? Bloggers, tweeters and other social media influencers who have their followers' ears. If you're one of those active influencers, it is thought that upwards of 70% of your followers will take what you say for granted. And Big Pharma, to cite just the one example, has grown accustomed to driving some of its content down to those influencers' doorsteps.

Apart from the reviews and other people's opinions that we seek in order to firm up our own positions on any subject, the latest and highly sophisticated phenomenon of "social media intelligence", i.e. that science −algorithm?- that tells us who is doing the influencing and who are being persuaded, the end product is an amazingly potent vehicle for valuable connections −of the commercial kind.

The key here is that there is no need for large outlays of funds to touch base with a specific audience or market. All you need to do is reach out to one of the agencies that specialize in social media intelligence, and they may be able to tell you where your ideal audience is, and who moves them. The impact of that on market research studies or new product launches is compelling, to say the least, for when it comes through your influencer, it's as good as a five-star review.

Naturally, the flip side of all that may be dangerous

to your product or service, and what you need to do so as not to be taken hostage by one opinion leader is spread your risk a little –get on the friendly side of more than the one. Beware of the competitor who is a step ahead of you.

The Wrong Influence

This may be of greater interest to parents, particularly those with teenage children.

In our anxiety-bloated world, parents can easily exert a bad influence on their children, no matter how loving they may be. One or both parents can smoke at a time when they're admonishing their children not to. They can drink, drive recklessly, separate, do street drugs, abuse prescription pills, abandon their children and do all kinds of other crazy things, frequently in full view of highly impressionable children. For many, life can be extremely rough, with people perpetuating acts of violence that traumatize other people existence and propel them to an existence riddled with despair. The ones who are most vulnerable are children and adolescents who, before they even have a chance at shaping their own destinies, have to endure the harsh bestiality of life at home.

Since none of us relish the idea of our children getting mired in any addiction, it follows that the practice to follow in our homes is to be categorical about the misery that abusing alcohol drugs can cause. But instead of communicating that message loud and clear, keeping our medicines out of reach and having frequent candid discussions about the ill effects of prescription and other drugs –i.e. instead of exerting our most positive influence- many parents are getting complacent. A recent study reveals that parents are not communicating the gravity involved in a teen stealing pills from a parent –or otherwise getting hold of some prescription drugs. And yet, research has revealed that one in four adults has used prescription drugs in their recent past. This has the magnitude of an epidemic amongst teens, while some parents continue treating the whole issue with marked indifference. They commit their children to a life of addiction because they are unwilling to face this topic that they find hard to talk about, or because of an ill-conceived notion that their children are above it all.

Teenage years are particularly difficult and can easily become emotionally upending, causing teenagers to seek relief by way of indulging in abusive behaviors, including alcohol and drugs, eating disorders and self-harming by way of cutting and burning. Teens carry this huge stigma of being physically clumsy, with frequent mood swings, bad-tempered, over-sensitive, unduly intense, attention grabbing and more. Add to that the fact that they go through what at times are exasperating hormonal changes, and it becomes odd that people can't understand why teens seek to drown their emotional pain with abusive behaviors. It is easier for people to simply blame teen moods as part of growing up.

Peers thus have an enormous influence to exert, and it can flip this way or that. Peers and "best friends" have more credibility than parents. They wield an enormous amount of influence. If at 15, your best friend drinks heavily, chances are you're going to drink heavily as well. And the problem with alcohol is that it almost invariably co-exists with other mental disorders, particularly depression, general anxiety disorder and, mostly for girls, eating disorders.

CHAPTER EIGHT
SELF-ESTEEM: THE HOUSE OF CARDS

Tread carefully if you're still on the self-esteem bandwagon or if you were pumped full of self-esteem, much like a bicycle tire, as you grew up. "Look," your parents would tell visiting family, "Johnny can already count to five!" That would be when you were two-years old, "Count to five Johnny so that Uncle Fred can see." Then Uncle Fred would pitch in with: "Wow, isn't Johnny the smartest boy!" And then when you grew up to age five or six, didn't your parents tell you –again, and for the millionth time- that you're the brightest of your age, and handsomest too? "Look," the same visiting uncle would be told, "Doesn't he look like a 10-

year old already?" And then, "He's the tallest for his age, and he's learning to play chess." Learning to play chess, everyone knows, is a sure sign of a superior brain! Finally, the worst would come a couple of years later, just prior to puberty, when you'd be told on a daily basis that you can be anything you want to be. "Look, Uncle Fred, Johnny can be just about anything he wants to be, and he's settled on being a brain surgeon or an astrophysicist when he grows up, haven't you, Johnny?"

It is good to remember that the concept of self-esteem, as aggrandized as we know it today, goes back only half a century, i.e. from the days when the flower people of the 60's and 70's confused loving their children with pumping them up with forbidding notions of grandeur.

Self-esteem has thus become the common yardstick by which we evaluate ourselves, and our parents enthusiastically outdo themselves in fostering it in us, believing -poor souls- that they're building us up for the uncertain times ahead.

There are two essential components to self-esteem:

1. A feeling of being generally competent and

comfortable to deal with whatever comes up

2. And a feeling of being worthy

The first of those two components is synonymous with the notion of being self-assured, giving ourselves high marks with regards to our abilities in general. Our specific skills don't necessarily come into the equation. More significant is our "fluid" intelligence, comprising our ability to interact well with our environment, this environment to include an endless amalgam of complex combinations of circumstances, people, surprise events etc. This assertion of self-efficacy is a measure of our evaluation of our own fluid intelligence. Since what is going on is all happening in the realm of the subconscious, we feel it only by way of self-assurance, better known as self-esteem.

The second component, involving the concept of worthiness, is more subjective and therefore more challenging. What are we meant to be worthy of? Are we meant to be worthy of society's acceptance, happiness, having the best family, doing great professionally, a leadership role in our community, material well being?

The measures for "worthy" or being deserving are numerous, and the relative impact of each part fluctuates with the dynamic nature of the whole. In addition, "worthy" can fluctuate with mood. It is easier to feel worthy when the mood is upbeat. Therefore, because it is possible that we are constantly evaluating our self-worthiness, figuring out what life has in store for us, then it is probably preferable to avoid "worthy" and replace it instead it with the more manageable self-respect.

Thus self-esteem entails the marks that we give ourselves in terms of our general capabilities as well as the degree to which we have self-respect.

But we know that it's not as simple as that, for both those elements are impacted considerably by our culture, faith, society's fads and factors like stereotyping, stigmas, guilt, upbringing, environmental and behavioral issues, and more.

For example, our self-assurance is developed in us within a certain environment or geography, where our familiarity with our surroundings plays an important role. In other words, we feel we can cope with whatever comes at us more effectively within the confines of our everyday setting. Thus if we move from the U.S. to India for example, much of the nurturing of our abilities and our interaction with American society may not necessarily be of help in India. Does that mean that our self-esteem depends on where we find ourselves at any given time? Does the same logic apply when we move from one trade or employer to another? One group of friends to a new one, younger/older, more/less sophisticated?

Our environment has a lot to say with regard to how we feel about ourselves, and our environment is not always predictable. We will come back to this issue when we discuss the "holistic" approach to self-esteem in the last section of this chapter.

Self-esteem v. self-compassion

Self-esteem is a delicate –frequently tantalizing- measure of how one is doing. Too much of it conjures up self-aggrandizement and arrogance, while too little of it beckons all kinds of problems, including fear, self-recrimination and different degrees of paralysis.

Self-esteem, or self-image, is not to be confused

with self-compassion. Of the two, many researchers believe that self-compassion that is the more advantageous to succeed out there in the material world. They feel that as long as you are at peace with yourself, you can self-train to achieve good results in business, with self-esteem playing a secondary and almost irrelevant role.

But it is self-esteem of course which is considered the overarching driver of success in Western cultures. The reasoning in the West has it that you must absolutely have a high assessment of yourself in order to get anywhere in business, or in a career. For example, can a sales person with a poor self-image make cold calls? Can they be effective in closing on deals –in actually asking for the contract or sale? Can a department head with low self-esteem wield the necessary degree of influence on people in other departments over whom he or she has not formal standing? Can someone with erratic self-esteem go up on a stage and make a presentation in front of 500 people?

One of the issues that high self-esteem individuals have is that they cannot perceive, or be perceived, wavering in their self-assessment. Once you fixate positively about yourself, there is almost no turning back, for the mere beginnings of self-doubt brings down the self-assessment. This makes you fragile and lacking in self-trust, which is again a downward pull. Self-doubt to a person with high self-esteem is a slippery slope that has got to be checked promptly before it overcomes the years of nurturing.

From another perspective, no matter how brilliant you are, there are always people who are more brilliant, and no matter how hard you try, there are always people who seem to attain the same results with less effort. There is always someone better looking, taller, richer, more eloquent and a higher-echelon leader. In fact, when the mood is such that we are being hard on ourselves, it is easy for us to perceive that there is always someone doing better than us and who makes us feel like a failure, and failure is forbidden when you're an avid member of the self-esteem religion. Failure, even temporary setbacks, risks to bring down the house of cards.

Besides, when you attain self-esteem, you have to keep it, which can be a daily struggle in the best of times. As such, you must keep stroking your ego and feeling that you are totally amazing, and then you must maintain that high mental image of yourself, for fear that any misstep could set you back in an ugly fashion.

This is why the notion has gained prominence that self-esteem is not what it's been proclaimed to be. It is one's own assessment of what one is worth, one's attitude towards oneself, but that need not be reflected by what other people think, or by advancement on the career ladder. It is subjective, some claim, and therefore does not deserve all the acclaim. You can think that you're just great, but that doesn't make you a better manager, leader, lover, friend, parent, or spouse. The poise you may muster may not be perceived as you imagine if, for example, you're being interviewed. In fact, the interviewer may react negatively at the slightest hint of arrogance.

Naturally, we don't particularly relish being impaired with low self-esteem either. What we can do is take the concept out of our consideration altogether and replace it with self-compassion.

Self-compassion is indeed more malleable, easier on the soul, more amenable to a prompt rebound after a setback and an all-in-all better key to unlocking your potential. It embodies a fundamental willingness to treat yourself kindly when in doubt, or having made mistakes. It then prompts you to slowly work yourself out of the whole −compassionately. In study after study, research has shown that self-compassion is a far better conduit to a personal sense of well being and happiness.

"Well," you might say to yourself, "I can't make cold calls. I never have." But the idea is that you accept that of yourself −compassionately- and determine to practice making cold calls until you improve at it −if, that is, it's meant for you to make cold calls. Your self-compassion played a critical role there in motivating you to do what you had to do, and to do it as well as possible.

In this line of thinking, self-compassion, or self-acceptance, goes beyond achievement and the workplace, to a whole new realm of goodness and happiness. Self-compassion thus is the bedrock of the balance you strive to attain in your life. Since you accept yourself compassionately, it probably follows that you accept others as well in the same manner, and that you are an optimist with an outgoing personality, all necessary ingredients for a well equilibrated approach to life.

We can create a simple comparison between self-compassion and self-esteem since we all make mistakes. In the case of a person with high self-esteem, mistakes can upset the person's delicate psychological make-up, whereas in the other case, a mistake is reason to embark on self-improvement –compassionately and without being too hard on oneself.

Have we just described someone whose standards are low and whose tolerance for mediocrity is high? Are self-compassionate individuals as happy with themselves irrespective of the quality of their performance? Are they pleased with whatever they do immaterial of the outcome? The short answer is no -not at all.

In the tests that researchers conducted, the people with self-compassion viewed their weaknesses as areas that they were going to work on with the view to creating improvements.

There was neither acceptance of their weaknesses nor of their poor output but, instead, there was resolve, with compassion, to improve. This determination would lead to greater work quality, rather than to a deterioration of self-esteem.

A self-accepting executive does not lose sight of the fact that he or she is accountable, and that they are responsible for what they produce. According to the research findings, of the two types of personalities, the self-compassionate executive is more likely to overcome obstacles and to reach the desired results.

One of the reasons for these findings is that the self-compassionate person, unlike the individual with high self-esteem, does not reflect endlessly over negative results. The self-image is preserved by the drive to rectify and do better, and there is little preoccupation with safeguarding the self-image or ego. It is difficult for the ego-conscious person to even admit that they've done wrong, never mind find motivation to correct the wrong.

The concept of self-esteem is thus fraught with associations with "ego" and "arrogance".

The holistic approach to self-evaluation

Self-esteem and the notion that "none of us are perfect" are frequently at odds with one another. Similarly, self-esteem and perfectionism are also in conflict. In fact, there are many factors that can prevent us from having high self-esteem. We may have been bullied or mentally or physically abused as a child and may have carried this chip through adolescence into adulthood. We may have just come into a society with the wrong skin color or accent or height -or other incongruities. Worse, we may have a disposition for one of the debilitating diseases or for depression. When it comes to self-esteem, depression is an almost insurmountable obstacle. It is difficult to think highly of oneself when one's energy is depleted and one's outlook dimmed.

And equally difficult is low self-esteem, however it comes into one's life. Low self-esteem is the harbinger of low self-compassion, and that has a vise-like hold that is very difficult to unwind. With low self-acceptance, one is harsh, unforgiving on oneself, and one loses all motivation for self-remedies. And it is at such low points in our lives that we risk acquiring deeply-set relational and emotional problems.

Those illnesses and frames of mind –and many more- may disqualify us from association with those with a high self-esteem; unless, of course, we work on improving ourselves in a holistic way.

The holistic way of life looks at a person as a whole: mind, body, and spirit. From that standpoint, a low level of self-esteem becomes a symptom within the whole body, and by caring for the whole body, the system can get cured. By enabling the person to gradually achieve optimal well-being, the person's self-acceptance can be revived. The person becomes responsible for continued balance in all everyday functions and choices. In this holistic way of life, the person takes charge with method and resolve.

Although the philosophy and practice of the holistic way are several millennia old, we were loudly alerted by Socrates who, in the fourth century BC proclaimed that "for the part can never be well unless the whole is well." In our context here, one cannot have a high level of self-esteem if the whole is not well.

Then the centuries flowed until came the development of antibiotics and the mass production of pharmaceuticals in the mid-20th century, and with that the heralding of Western traditional medicine at its highest acclaim. Disorders became subject to prompt cures, and people could disregard nutritious diets and healthy lifestyles.

From that point on it took several decades before people started realizing that the cures were frequently worse than the underlying diseases. Western traditional medicine had no patience for anything beyond the most acute of disorders and certainly no ready answer for anyone with multiple chronic diseases.

In the West, integrative medicine started gaining momentum after that, with many "complementary" modalities. In the East, the holistic approach had never waned throughout those periods.

In the holistic way, the earth's systems of air, land, animals, etc. are inseparable from the earth itself. What happens to one affects all others. Our notion of self-compassion, in the holistic way, is inseparable from all other parts of the person. In addition, the person is not in a vacuum but is constantly being influenced by the environment and by the behavior of others.

An executive readying himself or herself for a meeting with a top client would feel and perform better at the meeting if he or she had been maintaining a healthy lifestyle and feeling good about their overall energies. This healthy lifestyle includes a resolve to keep doing better, no matter how well balanced life seems to be at any given moment. When one is moving in the right direction, from a philosophical and practical point of view, one makes additional forward strides every time one encounters setbacks. Thus one's whole state of wellness and one's self-esteem are, indivisible. They move in tandem, perpetually reinforced by good health, emotional well being, and an optimistic frame of mind.

CHAPTER NINE
THE ROAD TO GREATNESS

In this chapter, The Road to Greatness, our emphasis is on "the road", rather than on "greatness". If we were to preach greatness to the exclusion of all else, we would place many peoples' mental well being in jeopardy. After all, who among us can cope with "greatness or nothing"?

Our second emphasis is that "the road" is comprised of one or two fundamental themes –usually one- that we hold dear to our hearts.

The question has been asked countless times in the past, and students of the subject as well as their coaches and mentors have argued endlessly on both sides of the equation. Are leaders born or made? Are some people born to become leaders while others, even with great effort, never rise beyond following? Or is leadership a skill that can actually be learned and employed by people who want to make a difference? Let us view this intriguing thought from a couple of practical perspectives.

We witnessed in an earlier chapter how Sir Winston Churchill had a unique megaphone, that of the BBC radio, which he used with extraordinary skill to influence millions of people around the globe. The point is this: Churchill's father was a luminary in his own right, a clever politician and a man of the pen. We can thus assume that Churchill was raised in a house full of books with a father, the patriarch, had considerable influence, all the way to the British Parliament. Can we therefore assume that Churchill grew up with a strong predisposition for being opinionated and thinking and speaking clearly? Was he brought up with an edge over other would-be leaders? Was he reared for leadership?

Naturally, you can also be inspirational without giving great speeches, much to the dismay of those who believe that great oratory is a must ingredient in the makings of a leader. Great oratory naturally helps a lot, but it is not a must, as can be demonstrated with Gandhi's example.

The Indian spiritual and political leader, Mahatma Gandhi (1869 - 1948), did not have any megaphone, and yet he changed the course of the future of India. He did that not so much with speeches, but with his unwavering beliefs of non-violence and attaining political goals through peaceful means. He was frequently jailed for his anti-war activism, and he retaliated with extended fasts in protest for political injustice. With a tiny skeletal figure that epitomized him famously worldwide, and always clad in the meekest of garments, Gandhi was able to influence hundreds of millions of people in India and globally – without any prowess at speech-making. In addition, we don't know much about the influences on Gandhi during his earlier years, but it would seem that this great leader made himself up from meek beginnings.

Let's shift the discussion for a moment from leader to theme –or calling.

If you were to think of a leader that you look up to, your mind would quickly focus on his or her theme. In his inaugural address, John F. Kennedy chose "Freedom" as his dominant theme. He visited several other concepts but always returned to freedom, so that historians remember his inaugural address as having been exceptionally on freedom. The other guideline that the "Freedom" address highlights is that it is best to stick to one dominant theme that followers will recall. However, being the great speaker that he was, JFK could have rattled off names from the phone book and would have been great at it. Not so with Nelson Mandela though. He was a great leader who couldn't make a decent speech if his life depended on it. His greatness came instead as a result of lifetime achievements on behalf of his people.

A principal theme or calling is the lightening rod that fills that void in your life and becomes your prime source of energy, motivation, inspiration and direction. It prods you forward from the moment you get up in the morning and sustains you through difficulties and seemingly insurmountable obstacles. And although no one can or should tell anyone else what precise calling or set of themes anyone should embrace, people can derive a good deal of encouragement while working on better shaping or crystallizing one's calling.

The alternative is not pretty. Drifting aimlessly through life's vagaries is like swimming against the current. You remain in place no matter how much you push and sweat. The visions of what you could have achieved would torture you and wreak havoc on your soul. No control and no direction end up with no motivation –nothing to aspire for. And being the bizarre human beings that we frequently are, we frequently put on disguises and dress up our hopelessness, lest people realize how weak we are. By drifting aimlessly, you thwart the potential you were given at birth.

It's also critical in shaping our lives not to allow others to pitch-in too fervently. One thing you can bet on is that there will be concerted efforts by others to do precisely that, efforts that will haunt you as you scramble to find your own parameters. At an early age, and as we saw in the preceding chapter, your parents and friends will have an endless array of prescriptions for your so-called happiness, and the prevailing social norms will pressure you endlessly as well: get a great job, get married, have children, get a house in the suburbs, join the Air Force like your dad did, and much more. In fact, if you don't exhibit fortitude of character and steadfastness, this stream of what society would have you do and be will follow you all the way to the grave.

Many people will in fact welcome having their purpose in life handed over to them on a silver platter. It is a relief for them not to have to struggle on a fundamental quest like that. That sense of relief will promptly vanish however when they discover that the purpose and existence they had espoused were anything but what they wanted for themselves. They thus become frustrated and diminished like wilted plants, their visions unfulfilled.

Do the best themes come when someone's on fire, or do they come as a result of passionate labor and development? Did Martin Luther King, Jr. start with the theme "I have a dream", or did he work his way up to it by feeling passionately about his people's plight? Naturally, we don't know how it came to him, but it is best to assume that it came to him at the right time in the right sequence after working tirelessly on other close themes.

And although we humans tend to connect mostly with our local networks and communities, the recent burgeoning of corporate takeovers, outsourcing and globalization has paved the way for a dramatic increase in the influence we exercise at a distance. Churchill did it through the BBC radio, and people are doing it in abundance through social media. Thus social media leaders are certainly not big-time speakers, and what posture they put on is immaterial. With them, the chase for followers is much more intense than in real life prior to Facebook and Twitter.

Is a leader born or made? Is charisma self-made? Can someone who does not have a booming voice succeed? How about someone who is just 5 feet tall? Here is how Vince Lombardi saw it: *"Leaders are made, they are not born. They are made by hard effort, which is the price which all of us must pay to achieve any goal that is worthwhile."*

The way we see it is that through inherited genes, and through the specific home influences during their developing years, some people can be advantageously disposed said to rise to the mark of greatness. However, and in confirmation of what Vince Lombardi had to say, it is likely that many more leaders start out as regular individuals who wanted to make something great out of their lives. They dared to pursue the visions that defined them with a passion that is not usually found among other people. They may not have all the necessary leadership skills at the onset but they pursued and learned from their mistakes and their experiences. They were committed to bringing the people they lead towards their goals. When they fail, they are the first to stand up and try again. They inspire their subordinates to do the same until their goal has been achieved.

A cautionary word: the search for your basic theme or calling should not be conducted with angst, as if something tangible is missing and you need to find it right away. Instead, you ought to think of your calling as your contribution to mankind, the amount of love you can muster and spread around, the amount of light you can diffuse on the darkness that permeates our universe, and the amount of healing you can dispense where it is vital. You can never go wrong hugging the virtues of love, kindness, and benevolence.

Humanity would not have reached the progress we enjoy now if man had only relied on the innate leadership of a very few number of people. Very few people start out with the modesty, compassion, and determination required to become a good leader. Many of the advancements we enjoy now are the fruits of the leadership of ordinary men who dreamed big for themselves and for their fellow men. These seemingly ordinary men worked hard to develop their leadership qualities that helped them inspire the people they worked with. They braved all the hardships required to achieve success in whatever field they chose to excel in.

Vision: the Tool to Sharpen

If you are reading this eBook and wondering if you were born a leader or not, you need to understand that you can become whatever you choose to become. Your efforts in learning how to become a better leader demonstrates that you have what it takes to become one. Many good leaders before you started out as simple, ordinary men. They all came from various circumstances – some were born into a rich family while others were born in poverty.

Some of them have multiple titles at the end of their names while others have barely attended any formal schooling. But they all had one thing in common – no matter what challenges they were facing, they found the courage to overcome those challenges to achieve success and make the world a better place at the same time. They all had a fire underneath them that kept them steeped in passion. With that knowledge, I hope that you now believe that you can transform yourself into some form of greatness that is within reach for you.

Greatness is all about getting from point A to point B. Leaders exist to direct a group of people to a better place. That better place can mean different things for different people. Leaders lead their people towards success, abundance, freedom or simple happiness. But the destination has to be absolutely clear to the leader himself in order for him to lead his subordinates to that new place.

`Would you tell me, please, which way I ought to go from here?' – said Alice in Wonderland.
`That depends a good deal on where you want to get to,' said the Cat.
`I don't much care where--' said Alice.
`Then it doesn't matter which way you go,' said the Cat.

The Cat in Alice in Wonderland clearly stated it. It

doesn't matter which way a leader goes if he or she doesn't care or doesn't know where he wants to go.

A good leader will only be able to discern the right path if he or she has a clear vision of the destination. That vision will enable the leader to build trust, teamwork, and motivation and shared responsibilities amongst his subordinates.

Along the way, you as a leader will have to face a lot of choices. You will have to make a lot of decisions not only for yourself but for your team as a whole. Having a clear vision will help you determine the right direction you and your team have to take. You would not need to wait for any sign or provocation from other people to move. You will be able to think for yourself and your team to find the ways, on how you can change your visions into reality.

Having a vision doesn't just mean defining the ultimate goal you want to achieve. To achieve relative greatness, your vision should encompass more than the dream itself. It should include an extensive knowledge of who you and your team are. What are your strengths? What are your weaknesses? Do you and your team lack any skills that will help you achieve your goals? Do you and your team need to work on eliminating some weaknesses that may hinder you from making your vision a reality? You need to know what values are important for you and your team.

You also need to remember that your vision is something that you need to keep alive. It is not enough that you lay it out to your team in the beginning. It is important to remind them about it every day so they will not lose focus on what is important for your team. The more you and your team are able to focus on your goals, the clearer the vision becomes and the deeper it stays in their hearts.

It is not easy to achieve greatness, even in its modest form. It requires hard work. Here is how the great poet Henry Wadsworth Longfellow wrote in his inimitable style:

The heights by great men reached and kept
Were not attained by sudden flight,
But they, while their companions slept,
Were toiling upward in the night.

Once you have identified the vision you want to turn into reality, push yourself to live it at once. You need to act as if whatever you have envisioned is already happening. Your daily actions should be in harmony with your vision. And when your subordinates and the other people you deal with see you living the dream, they will then believe how serious you are with your vision. Seeing your commitment to the dream, the people around you will also feel committed to achieving it. Your passion and commitment are contagious, so be discerning with what you pass around.

What matters the most to each of us defines us. For many, the pleasures that frame us surround us for all who can see to see, for all who can smell and touch to feel. One such pleasure may be to take one's family or friends and splash barefoot in the crystal clear waters of a naked stream, or to go unaccompanied to the depths of the ocean and discover the thousand ornaments of a coral reef. Nature has indeed been the inspiration for man for thousands of years, and when you are in search of your own passion, you can take temporary refuge in nature's unending bounty.

Love is another place where you can be absolutely safe and rewarded. Love is not a circle with strict confines but rather an open-ended fusion with large and small creatures, with nature, with the cosmos and with Man's past and future predicaments. And where you never before outlined what is required of you in terms of love, you ought to spend time each day reflecting on love. When you are filled with love, you acquire an overarching glow under which your calling comes to life –and so do your followers. Of all the contagious themes, love is the most potent.

Love, thoughtfulness and compassion thus constitute the necessary framework for molding your specific calling. A calling or life purpose becomes your preferred way of making your contributions, each contribution bearing the hallmark of someone with purpose, someone who can indeed withstand the current. From that framework of being at peace with the world everything else flows, and eventually the glow that surrounds you will engulf the manifestations of your life purpose in the other aspects of your lives, such as career, relationships and lifestyle.

You can't focus on the manifestations –career, relationships and other- in an attempt to derive a clearer overall calling. That would be like picking up a wild flower and trying to put additional petals on it. Conversely, by dedication to the cause of love and respect, all the details of your calling will become evident, including career, relationships, community affairs, and other issues of mind, body and soul.

We all have dreams, although unfortunately they are often opaque and not easy to discern. They are also frequently of changing looks, at times appearing what they were not originally meant to be. You thus lose confidence in your dreams, and they end up being discarded. Your dreams are not always to be invented, but rather to be discovered. However you cannot discover any dreams if you are not of the correct mindset, open to the influences gained by your virtues and preparation. Open yourself up to love of nature –to love. It will elevate you to where things are clearer.

I close this chapter with two Guidelines for Going from "goal" to "calling":

1. When you are striving and struggling for a particular goal, you do well –always- to think not of the prize or wealth you would amass at the end, but of how the project would impact your character. If

you deem that the impact would be positive, that would beckon you to move forward.

2. When you are striving and struggling for a particular goal but are not sure whether its impact on your character would be positive, you would do well to take a step backwards and visualize the anticipated proceedings. You would need to focus on all of the project's milestones and gage how well you would cope at every stage, not from the point of view of necessary effort, but from that of whether you would remain true to your values.

I'll close this chapter with:

10 Guidelines to keep the fire burning

1. You need to allow love and compassion to be your guiding light in life: love people, love nature, love to feel and touch and allow others to love you in return. Have we mentioned that enough times? You must render yourself "available" to the goodness that surrounds you.

2. Help people whenever you can. Volunteer, teach, mentor. Nothing is more precious than this type of giving, and nothing is more rewarding than mentoring in particular. Set your mind on finding situations that will permit you to mentor someone or a group of people.

3. When you are striving and struggling for a particular goal, you do well –always- to think not of the prize or wealth you would amass at the end, but of how the project would impact your character. If you deem that the impact would be positive, that would beckon you to move forward.

4. When you are striving and struggling for a particular goal but are not sure whether its impact on your character would be positive, you would do well to take a step backwards and visualize the anticipated proceedings. You would need to focus on all of the project's thresholds and gage how well you would cope at every stage, not from the point of view of

necessary effort, but from that of whether you would remain true to your values.

5. You have to take care of your health: good nutrition, good hydration, plenty of sleep, plenty of exercise, a schedule that includes ample socializing and laughter. Laughter is a huge "uplifter" and stabilizer of hypertension (high blood pressure) and other ailments brought about by stress. Teach yourself to laugh out loud and as frequently as you can.

6. You need to keep track of all the stressors that impact your life and deal with those by confronting the underlying issues and avoiding denial. The healthy lifestyle described above should take care of most stressors. Meditation, visualization, breathing and other techniques are also highly advisable. Seek out the stress-relief modality that best suits your temperament and environment and become adept at it.

7. Imagine yourself in a very pleasant situation

where things are going your way, and all the outcomes are pleasant (For example, imagine that you are going to ace the pending exam, and imagine the happiness that would result. You can be hopeful most of the time if you think of yourself as successful.

8. When you feel stuck and find yourself in a depressive "rut", it is good to invoke "pattern interrupts" to help you out. You can achieve that by doing something unexpected, like climbing on a table and lifting a leg. By harnessing the power of surprise, you would tell your brain to switch to more pleasant thinking)

9. Learn to trust and nurture your intuition by following your gut. People like Steve Jobs and Bill Gates could have never done all what they did without the help of sharpened instincts that allowed them to take intuitive shortcuts and make quantum leaps forward at every turn. Faced with a few options, next time just go with the option that "feels right". That's what your

instinct would have been telling you.

Socialize, network and stay close to friends and family. Nothing leads to negative thinking more than isolating yourself, and the more interaction you have with people you love, the better off you will be.

CHAPTER TEN
THE MANY FACES OF LEADERSHIP

The first rule of leadership is that you don't have to look or behave like Zeus (The Greek father of the gods and men, and god of the sky and thunder) in order to rise to the order of leader. All you need to be, for example, is a Project Manager, with a team of 10 or 15 people, assigned to an all-important task. That would make you a team leader "on the ascent", for if you do well, your net will be cast over many more teammates.

You can be fat and short and have a heavy lisp in your voice and still become a leader, providing you have something to offer.

We are trying here to get away from our classical and outmoded thinking about leadership. That model would require you to possess a slew of vital traits such as charisma, decisiveness, intelligence, clarity of thought and voice, wisdom, empathy, compassion and many more.

And while these characteristics are admirable and would certainly enhance any leader's expansionist goals, they are simply too difficult to attain as a whole. Thus for those of us who are imperfect, our chances are not entirely dim, and those who have set the example of being flawed in the past are, if anything, more numerous than the perfect model.

Thus a leader is usually, but not inevitably, someone with an array of ethical and related qualities. These qualities are neither necessary nor sufficient, but at least some may commonly be found in the persona of a "utopian" leader.

Apart from accomplishments and traits that may qualify a leader, there are literally hundreds of different types of leaders: athletic leaders who push their teams to excellence, trail-blazing academics with cutting-edge laboratory research, scientists like Thomas Edison and

Albert Einstein, military leaders like Field Marshal Bernard Montgomery who defeated Erwin Rommel, aka the Desert Fox, at El-Alamein, 5-star General Dwight Eisenhower, the Supreme Commander of Allied forces on D-Day, spiritual gurus like the Dalai Lama and the Pope, political leaders like Churchill and JFK and motivational speakers like Tony Robbins, to name but a few.

We have to also point out that apart from there being various types of leaders, there are many levels within each grouping. The size of the flock used to be a reliable barometer as to the level of leadership exercised by a specific leader until the advent of social media. With some folks amassing followers by the half-million and by the millions, betrothing their likes to people that no one ever perceives outside of Twitter and FB, and with others going viral overnight, the number of followers has taken a hit as a barometer of grandeur. For example, outside of social media, we used to be able to say that the Catholic Cardinal of New York is a religious leader with, let's say, a million followers, while The Pope easily exceeds that, with many more followers. That placed the Pope on a higher echelon than the Cardinal.

Similarly, a person can be a huge leader in two different domains. The good example there would be Bill Gates who pioneered in software when he became a huge magnet at Microsoft, only to later become, yet again, a huge leader in philanthropy. If you don't believe that, watch some videos of how he is received in African townships where his foundation has brought in water, medicines and particularly vaccines.

The same with most Presidents of the United States. They lead as Presidents, and then they lead again as do-gooders. Presidents Bill Clinton and Jimmy Carter are prime examples of that dual leadership role.

The final part of this brief introduction of ours has to do with what it takes –or does not take- to rise to the level of leader in modern America.

A great leader may have at least some grand qualities. Yet not every great leader becomes a legendary leader. That post is reserved for the very few. What turns some of the leaders to the great among the greatest? Three answers there: the nature of their calling and how many that can serve (e.g. Gandhi at a time of great political injustice), the need for their services (e.g. at a time of war or drought or famine) and their particular uniqueness, as orators for example (Churchill and Martin Luther king Jr.) or as inspirational (e.g. Tony Robbins, Sir Richard Branson, Deepak Chopra). Every leader has something unique about them which, when developed, can propel them to the ranks of the greats. Sometimes they have that one – or two- great things going for them, such as with the great penmanship and speech-giving prowess of the great Churchill.

Must a leader always lead by example? Surely the answer to that is a resounding no –at least not always. Many leaders lead by example, while for others, it is strictly "do as I say, not as I do".

Can a leader be obese? Short? We saw in an earlier chapter that indeed he can. The example we gave at the time was that of Sir Winston Churchill –again!- who, if one acknowledged that he'd been greatly instrumental in defeating fascism, one would have to say that he in fact he was the leader who saved the world from totalitarianism and subservience . And yet, he was anything but a model of athleticism, sobriety or other niceties. There was a good example of "do as I say, not as I do."

Napoleon Bonaparte (1761 – 1821) was the French military leader and emperor who conquered the whole of Europe. He was shrewd, ambitious and a genius at military strategizing, but he was also short as a stub and didn't look the least bit charismatic.

And the list goes on littered with anachronisms that belie what we've been told about leadership in the more conventional circles.

The truth is of course that you can wield influence if you're less than perfect. In fact, followers would probably like you more if you're less than utterly perfect in the Herculean sense –or one who does no wrong. That would be immensely intimidating to one and all.

The other truth is that people wield influence in different ways and for different purposes, and the way people wield it has a lot to do with their purpose.

For example, Steve Jobs was emblematic of a leader who leads by example. He had a manic obsession about miniaturizing. He kept bullying his engineers and suppliers until...you got it: he accomplished the best exploits in miniaturization since the earth detached from bigger masses after the Big Bang of four billion years ago.

He was by far one of the most enigmatic leaders of his time, leading his flock through an endless succession of pinnacles and so, who cares if he had flaws? Of course he had flaws, the kinds that are probably necessary for greatness.

He was thought to be somewhat gruff at work, a little bit of an intimidator, but that never stopped him. He was the embodiment of the manager who exerts unmatched influence. Let's examine some of his individual traits:

- He exuded confidence and was able to initiate change and inspire a shared vision

- He was absolutely expert at what he did, mastering his countless engineering and computer science topics

- He was super charismatic

- Worked tirelessly and had a knack for overcoming resistance or foot-dragging –by engineers, employees, suppliers, advertisers

- He gave the tasks that he delegated critical

significance so as to ensure that he got a best effort from those that he delegated to

- Every employee of his ended up revering Steve Jobs, irrespective of how hard he drove them

- They revered him in part because they saw how hard he drove himself

This was a case where he couldn't have done it if he didn't lead by example. The more he pushed himself, the more he asked of his flock. And as soon as his latest products started coming out, the leverage that Steve Jobs wielded began to stretch out from his own labs and setups to wherever else he ventured: whether in pursuit of licensing agreements, talks with competitors, seeking new outsourcing horizons, being invited to sit on other people's boardrooms, talks with banks and people in government. The world opened up to him, and each step increased his sphere of influence and brought additional leverage.

From another perspective, since the start of documented history, we have been blessed with legendary leaders that we have dubbed "the Greats" in this book. These leaders led their people effectively and made their masses believe and love them. Naturally, one of the marks of a great leader is how well history perceives him decades or centuries later. Many such leaders turned out to be so great that even today they are respected, remembered and taught in schools all over the world.

These magnificent men and women ushered their masses into new worlds, new beginnings and new ways of thinking. Right from the time of the ancient Egyptian Civilization to today's modern world there have been a succession of great leaders, such as Buddha, Hatshepsut, Alexander, Asoka, Louis XIV, Akbar, Gandhi, Martin Luther King, and many more. And even now, when time has moved on and there have been new civilizations and new cultures, the contributions of these ancient as well as more recent giants appear fresh and relevant, as if etched on our minds in the recent past.

Let us look at some of the most influential and impactful leaders who with their leadership qualities changed the theory of being a leader.

The Prophet Muhammad

One of the greatest medieval leaders, the Prophet

Muhammad led over one of the most widespread religions of all times, uniting his people in the process and bringing to his flock a range of humanitarian, social and religious disciplines to replace the chaos that reigned at the time. He was the creator of Islam and helped his followers to spread to all corners of the world. His contributions to broadening the reach of Islam are still ongoing, with the religion attaining the number one or two in numbers among religions in the world. He was also a philosopher, teacher and mentor who helped his people out of persecution and led some of the largest migrations in human history. He led many successful wars and defeated and conquered larger armies only with his legendary leadership qualities. The qualities that the Prophet Muhammad exhibited were those of courage, bravery, leading by example, clarity of purpose, persistence and military decisiveness.

Julius Caesar

Of all the emperors that ever lived, none was as important to his time as Caesar. You can get a measure of the importance of this man by the fact that he was not only one of the greatest military leaders but also one of the shrewdest political leaders ever. He fought many battles, led several victorious campaigns and increased the territory of the Roman Empire making it one of the most prosperous dynasties ever. In addition, Caesar revolutionized the Roman government and laid the foundation for an expanded Roman Empire. "Rome" at the time of Caesar spelled doom to his enemies and offered bountiful rewards to soldiers and the elite. In Caesar we have an example of a legendary leader with known characteristics of audacity, boldness, and charisma over his armies and people. Like Napoleon who followed so many centuries later, Caesar set new standards in military strategizing.

Mahatma Gandhi

Naturally, you can also be inspirational without giving great speeches. The Indian spiritual and political leader, Mahatma Gandhi (1869 - 1948), did not have any megaphone, and yet he changed the course of the future of India. He did that not so much with speeches, but with his unwavering beliefs of non-violence and attaining political goals through peaceful means. He was frequently jailed for his anti-war activism and on extended fasts in protests for political injustice, and he fervently disavowed himself from materialism. With a tiny skeletal figure that epitomized him famously worldwide, and always clad in the meekest of garments, Gandhi was able to influence hundreds of millions of people in India (which then included Pakistan as well).

This giant led his flock out of the clutches of the British Empire. He was originally named Mohandas Karamchand Gandhi, but due to his immense works and leadership, he came to be known as Mahatma, aka the great soul. In this example of leadership, an ordinary boy became extraordinary by developing a single-minded passion to free his people and give them independence. Gandhi was the highest possible emblem of leading by example, starving himself for months on end to score a point with his oppressors. He achieved all that by espousing non-violence, much like, more than a century later, how Martin Luther King Jr. went about his mission. Gandhi finally attained his ultimate goal when he led India to independence in 1947.

Mao Zedong

The founder of Maoism, Mao was the leader of the Chinese Revolution and the founding father of the

People's Republic of China. He successfully repelled the Japanese armies in the invasion of WWII and led China on the path to industrialization and economic revival. The case can easily be made that he laid the foundation for the superpower that China is today.

Nelson Mandela

Mandela is the latest of the modern-day heroes and legendary leaders. For 26 years he endured prison on behalf of his people when he could have easily compromised on his principles and made deals that with his captors that would give him his freedom. The first South African President who got elected in a fully democratic election, Mandela fought with all his might against the two-tier system of apartheid that regarded blacks as inferior to whites. He devoted his life and legacy to attaining freedom and equality for everyone in his beloved South Africa. His type of leadership did not include speech-making prowess, not did other characteristics really matter other than his devotion to his people, his determination, perseverance and courage and personal sacrifice. Note how this self-sacrificing trait recurs often as part and parcel of the trademarks of big-time leaders.

George Washington

What more can you say about someone other than to say that he was one of the four founders of our great nation. Without him and the without legacy he left us all, no one can really tell how America would have developed. George Washington was absolutely instrumental in putting his entire slew of visions on the line in what became the Constitution. He and others close to him had to envision not only what was best, but also what was practical and withstand the test of time. He etched his place in history as both Leader of the American Revolution and also the first President of the United States of America. Note that in this case many of the traits that a leader could benefit from existed in this man: foresight, vision and planning, his ability to lead and influence people and his moral standing among his soldiers. We discussed earlier the virtues of the High Road. Well, nobody hugged the high road tighter than George Washington.

Abraham Lincoln

Another giant among giants, Abraham Lincoln, one of the most legendary leaders of all times, left an indelible mark on his times as well as modern times. Lincoln was the 16th president of the United States, and he was considered the most intellectually brilliant of all the Presidents that followed. His epic struggles and toils for the country can act as inspiration for any person who followed in his tracks, particularly in the military field as well as that of government and politics. At the time of the Civil War, what was needed was a man of his stature and intellect to ensure that the country was not split into South and North. He also ended slavery by signing the Emancipation Proclamation and thus made himself the hero that all people loved in the country. In a twist of fate that the entire country mourned, Lincoln was assassinated, leaving behind an inimitable legacy what a leader should possess: Clarity of mission, determination, perseverance, and strongest sense of national pride.

Fidel Castro

Another strong though controversial leader, Fidel Castro led the Cuban Revolution and became President of Cuba for the entire period 1976 to 2008, one of the longest of any ruler at the head of his country's government. He rallied his countrymen out of chaos and dispersion into an entity with strong national pride. In 1962, Castro benefited from a misadventure of the CIA knows as the Bay of Pigs in which the CIA led some Cuban immigrants in the U.S. on a futile invasion of Cuba. As a result, he became an international hero and consolidated his hold over Cuba. The following year, in 1963, Russian missiles that were positioned in Cuba became the focal point of a nuclear standoff between the US and Russia that had the whole world fearful of an imminent nuclear holocaust. Castro recently relegated the Presidency to his brother. With Castro we have a leader whose main leadership traits consisted of charisma, bravura, a very strong will and strong personality, and a massive hatred for American politicians.

There are many common characteristics between many of the above legendary leaders, principally a very clear mind as to what they want, "a spine like a rod and back of steel", determination, the willingness for self-sacrifice for the cause, charisma, farsighted vision, and the smarts that go along with all that.

The fact that we had picked "legendary" leaders, i.e. heroes who withstood the test of time, should not persuade us that all leaders must rise to that level. We gave earlier a good example, and we will repeat it here: a Project Manager with 10 to 15 team members is a leader. We specifically called him or her a leader "on the ascent", for leaders rise and fall with the increase or decrease in their popularity, and our Project Manager, we deemed, could only go higher.

CONCLUSION

Of all the marks of leadership in everyday life at home and at the office, the ones that strike me as being the most essential to make you look and feel good, and to leave an imprint on your relationships are not 5, not 7, nor are they 10. They are only 3, and if you are the Project Manager on a critical assignment with a small team of "reports", or a Division Head when your company is downsizing or incurring massive change, these 3 will take you up the first hill from which you can see clearer. Those 3 traits that I value so much in our down-to-earth environment are:

1. **Love is by far the most essential**: love for yourself which we referred to as self-compassion, love for the people around you, whether you know them or not, and love for nature and the rest of the ecological system. Love is the perfect antidote to the fear-based world we live in. Love will help you reach within yourself for that spirituality that lies dormant inside of you and that can lift you up to levels that are hard to imagine. Love is also the perfect medicine for stress, for love brings about a

greater degree of socializing and laughter with friends, both activities known for their powerful anti-stress powers.

2. **Finding your purpose** (aka theme or calling) would be my second vital characteristic. Purpose is the lightening rod that fills that void in your lives and becomes your prime source of energy, motivation, inspiration and direction. It prods you forward from the moment you get up in the morning and sustains you through difficulties and seemingly insurmountable obstacles.

Remember how we asked the question whether the "I have a dream" theme came to MLK, or whether he worked at it day and night until it made sense and became his outcry to the world? To acquire a theme, you have to pick at your passions until something clicks in place. A life theme starts in the middle and is worked outwards until it becomes you, until you become totally identifiable with the theme, whatever that may be. If you think intensely about something, all kinds of goodies come to the fore that you never imagined would be there for you. Just do it and you will see.

3. **"Fit for life"** is my third critical characteristic that boosts every would-be leader's aspirations. I am propelled in that direction by two factors that eat away at our health: stress and our modern lifestyles, and I'll start with the latter:

Our grandparents and their generations used to eat wholesome foods, mostly raw food, a lot of grains and meat from free-ranging beef and poultry. What we have succumbed to these days is an addiction to the fast and the convenient, foods that are heavily processed and that contain dyes, preservatives, coloring flavors and a host of other chemicals that extend the food's shelf life. As for the beef and poultry, our farms are feeding them intolerable amounts of antibiotics to make them fatter and free from sickness. These antibiotics find their way into our systems, causing an ongoing epidemic in the U.S. So, pay attention to your diets, exercise regularly, stay hydrated, and make yourself get at least 8 or 9 hours' sleep at night. That would be "fit for life".

Fit for life also happens to be the best way to combat stress. You don't feel particularly stressed after a 2-mile run. Stress is pervasive in insidious ways. Oh the baggage we carry with us, the dead weight that gives us the crouch in our posture and the strain in the brain. Guilt is a lifetime companion that latches on even before we are born –much like a concentrate seeping down from the mother's womb to lodge in our embryonic heads. We then proceed to accumulate layer after layer of it, unaware of its torturous ways. Even as infants, four and five-year olds, we are made to feel guilt for misfortunes that we never even get to comprehend. And as we grow up, all kinds of "stressors" pile on: inherited predispositions to anxiety and disease, psychological, family and cultural-related stressors, not to mention employment and financial stress. The twin-headed monster of guilt and stress hides inside us like a sticky parasite that becomes hard to dislodge.

Apart from keeping fit, the other commendable lifestyle behavior is to not succumb to leanings towards isolation and, instead, to network and socialize as much as possible, trying always to find new friends and groups that can widen your knowledge and horizons.

Dear readers, I hope you had fun through the pages. I tried to give you leadership from a conventional perspective, as when I discussed the legendary "greats", as well as from a practical viewpoint, citing –more than once- the example of the Project Manager at the workplace. I sincerely hope each one of you found a precious take-away.